Licensing Occupations

Licensing Occupations

Ensuring Quality or Restricting Competition?

Morris M. Kleiner

2006

W.E. Upjohn Institute for Employment Research
Kalamazoo, Michigan

Library of Congress Cataloging-in-Publication Data

Kleiner, Morris M.
  Licensing occupations: ensuring quality or restricting competition? / Morris M.
  Kleiner.
    p. cm.
  Includes bibliographical references and index.
  ISBN-13: 978-0-88099-284-8 (pbk. : alk. paper)
  ISBN-10: 0-88099-284-0 (pbk. : alk. paper)
  ISBN-13: 978-0-88099-285-5 (hardcover : alk. paper)
  ISBN-10: 0-88099-285-9 (hardcover : alk. paper)
  1. Professions—Licenses—United States. 2. Occupations—Licenses—United States.
  3. Quality assurance—United States. 4. Competition—United States. I. Title.
  HD3630.U7K575 2005
  061'.3—dc22

                        2005028269

The facts presented in this study and the observations and viewpoints expressed are
the sole responsibility of the authors. They do not necessarily represent positions of
the W.E. Upjohn Institute for Employment Research.

Cover design by Alcorn Publication Design.
Index prepared by Diane Worden.
Printed in the United States of America.
Printed on recycled paper.

Contents

Figures

Tables

Acknowledgments

In writing this book I have benefited from the contributions of many individuals to whom I am most grateful. For most valuable assistance with the research I thank Irma Arteaga, Alexandra Broat, Joan Gieseke, Adrienne Howard, Alexander Lefter, John Linder, Claire Matese, Clint Pecenka, Keith Vargo, Yingying Wang, Brenda Wolfe, and Marie Zimmerman. I want to especially thank Hwikwon Ham for his dedication to and outstanding assistance on the project. The staff at the Industrial Relations Center's Herman Reference Room at the University of Minnesota and the Research Department at the Minneapolis Federal Reserve Bank provided valued assistance.

Useful comments on various parts of this book were provided to me by many of my colleagues, and I am particularly grateful to Leah Platt Boustan, Pam Brinegar, Richard Freeman, Mark Herzendorf, Francis Kramarz, Robert Kudrle, David Metcalf, James Nobles, Timothy Taylor, and Charles Wheelan. I want to especially thank Steven Tenn who read and commented on the entire manuscript and provided great insights. Participants in seminars at the Department of Justice, the Federal Trade Commission, Harvard University, Iowa State University, Kansas State University, London School of Economics, the National Bureau of Economic Research, Princeton University, the University of Chicago, the University of Melbourne, the University of Minnesota, and the W.E. Upjohn Institute for Employment Research provided useful suggestions that improved the book.

The staff at the W.E. Upjohn Institute for Employment Research was most helpful in funding the project, publishing the results, and providing valuable comments throughout the research process. I am most grateful to Randall Eberts, Bob Wathen, and Richard Wyrwa for their excellent comments on earlier drafts. I want to thank the staff at the National Bureau of Economic Research, especially Susan Colligan, for their cooperation on the project.

Lastly, I want to thank my family for their patience while I worked on this book. I also especially thank Sally M. Kleiner for her valuable assistance with many of the technical aspects of the project.

Preface

The licensing of occupations has a long and varied history. Among the oldest evidence of rules governing occupations is the existence of the Babylonian Code of Hammurabi, dating to around 1780 BCE. This body of codes stipulated both the fees patients were to pay for medical services and the punishments practitioners were subject to for negligent treatment. The medieval guilds of Europe form perhaps the most often-cited example of the imposition of tough restrictions on entering a craft or occupation. In the United States, through much of the nineteenth century, few restrictions were imposed on occupations that we normally think of as licensed, such as doctors or lawyers. During the past 50 years, however, with the increase in complexity of jobs, especially in the service sector, the licensing of individuals in these occupations has emerged as one of the fastest-growing labor market institutions in the United States and other industrialized nations.

Academics and policymakers have examined whether workers, consumers, practitioners, or society benefits from the regulation of occupations. As other labor market institutions such as unions have declined as a percentage of the workforce, the new guilds (as some have called licensed occupations) have grown. In this book, I attempt to answer some of the following questions: Why is occupational licensing a growing labor market institution? Who gains from this form of regulation? Do members of the occupation receive higher prices and earnings for their services as a result of regulation? Is the quality of service to consumers enhanced through the additional training and scrutiny of practitioners that licensing requires? Does the impact of licensing in the United States differ from that in Europe? Are there net economic benefits to occupational licensing? Why are practitioners often the driving force behind occupational regulation? Are there policy alternatives to occupational licensing?

The answers to these difficult questions are not made easier by the large amount of published material from economics, political science, history, law, psychology, and sociology on these topics. Although this book touches on all the disciplines that have delved into the topic of occupational licensing, its focus is on policy analysis, using economics and statistical methods. The book attempts to present a systematic discussion of the major benefits and costs of occupational licensing to the economies of the United States and several European countries. It follows that the reader must bring some knowledge of economics and statistics to the analysis of the topic. The general reader without this background will have no difficulty getting through the major portions of the book. Nevertheless, in places, I have brought in specialized material and directed the exposition to the specialist in economics and policy analysis.

xiii

Here the general reader may feel like a guest at a family party. When, after po-
lite general conversation, the family turns to narrow, immediate concerns, the
guest is left out of the loop of conversation. At such places, the reader should
judiciously push on, since the key elements of the book can be understood
without a technical background.

Morris M. Kleiner

1
Introduction and Overview

Dentists, doctors, lawyers, fortune tellers, and frog farmers are now licensed occupations in either all or some U.S. states.[1] During the early 1950s, only about 4.5 percent of the labor force was covered by licensing laws at the state level. That number had grown to almost 18 percent of the U.S. workforce in the late 1980s, with an even larger number if city and county licenses for occupations are included (Kleiner 1990). The number and percent of licensed occupations has continued to grow. Data from the Labor Market Information Survey and the 2000 census showed that the number of workers in occupations licensed by states in 2000 grew by 11 percent during the past 15 years to approximately 20 percent of the workforce.[2]

The reasons given for the growth and benefits of this form of regulation usually include the idea that existence of licenses may minimize consumer uncertainty over the quality of the licensed service and increase the overall demand for the service (Arrow 1971). However, in some cases, poor quality has larger social implications. A doctor who makes a bad diagnosis may cause a widespread epidemic. A boilermaker who installs a furnace incorrectly may cause a building to catch fire, which could result in the death of many people. In this sense, regulations that require a practitioner to be trained at a minimum level may produce positive social payoffs. Consumers often value the reduction in downside risk more than they value the benefits of a positive outcome. This consumer preference for the reduction of the risk of a highly negative outcome has been called "loss aversion" by Kahneman and Tversky (1979).

The general issue of licensing is often thought of in the context of most people's general experience with getting a driver's license (Camerer et al. 2003). In the case of driver's licenses, there are generally no supply limits that may drive up the benefits to a group of citizens, and the tests and requirements for the license are generally low. Most people would argue that driver's licenses are a good idea because a person cannot control who is driving on the road next to them and would like some assurance that the other individuals on the road are at least minimally competent. In contrast with licensing drivers, the entry costs of occupational licensing are generally high. Many years of schooling are often required, as are classes focused on professional training and tests that are often difficult to pass and given infrequently. Moreover, in the case of regulated occupations (e.g., doctors, dentists, and cosmetologists), the consumer has the ability to choose a service based on the perceived quality and service price but no ability to choose an unregulated practitioner. Whereas motor vehicle licensing has few costs and many benefits, the licensing of occupations is often perceived as providing few benefits to consumers and possibly imposing large costs.

A recurring issue for the public, policymakers, and economists has been deciding how government regulation of occupations impacts who works and how the work should be conducted. Usually such regulations require some demonstration of a minimum degree of competency to serve the public, and they specify a means to address negligence by service providers. Overall, these requirements are intended to have beneficial effects for consumers by increasing the quality of service. Individuals in these regulated occupations gain standardized work requirements and an increased demand for their services. This book examines the impact of occupational licensing on who gets to work in the licensed occupations. It focuses on the question of whether this labor market institution results in consumers receiving higher-quality services, as well as if there are enhanced earnings for practitioners and higher prices for consumers. The book presents new analysis and evidence on the productivity effects of licensing while detailing its price and labor market impacts. The evaluation of licensing focuses on the labor market impacts on the earnings and employment of regulated practitioners relative to similar unregulated practitioners. The data examined use information on licensing in the United States and give some comparisons for several of the larger nations in the European Union (EU), namely France, Germany, and the United Kingdom (UK). Policy options for regulating occupations in light of the findings are presented in the final chapter.

LICENSING: A HISTORICAL PERSPECTIVE

The study of the regulation of occupations has a long and distinguished tradition in the study of the labor market. Licensing was discussed by Adam Smith in the *Wealth of Nations,* where he focuses on the ability of the crafts to lengthen apprenticeship programs and limit the number of apprentices per master, thereby ensuring higher earnings for persons in these occupations (Smith 1937, Book I, Chapter 10, Part II). A part of Milton Friedman's dissertation focused on licensing, and he collaborated with fellow Nobel Laureate Simon Kuznets to coauthor *Income from Independent Professional Practice,* which examined the impact of licensing in the medical profession and compared it to licensing in the dental profession (Friedman and Kuznets 1945). During the 1960s the National Bureau of Economic Research's *Aspects of Labor Economics,* which presented the major works and important issues in labor economics, had a study of licensing as its lead article (Lewis 1962). In 1980 the American Enterprise Institute published *Occupational Licensure and Regulation,* which concluded with an assessment that occupational regulation had a positive effect on practitioners, but that it had a negative impact on consumers (Rottenberg 1980).

Recently there have been few studies detailing the effects of occupational licensing. Perhaps this lack of recent analysis is because the topic lies at the intersection of labor economics, law, and industrial organization and thus does not fit easily within one of the subfields of the social sciences as they have evolved. The reason for the lack of study is not because occupational licensing is on the decline. Using data from the census, Table 1.1 shows that, for the period 1990–2000, some of the largest licensed occupations (accountants, doctors, dentists, elementary school teachers, secondary school teachers, lawyers, and cosmetologists) showed considerable variation in employment growth. For example, the labor force grew by 13.2 percent over the decade, the number of doctors grew by 23.6 percent, and the number of lawyers grew by more than 24 percent. In contrast, the number of dentists and hairdressers and cosmetologists remained constant even though the U.S. population grew.

Consistent with general growth in wage inequality over the period, the greatest wage growth occurred in licensed occupations with the

Table 1.1 Employment and Wages (in nominal dollars) in Major Licensed Occupations, 1990–2000

	Employment			Hourly wage ($)			Hourly earnings ($)		
	1990	2000	% change	1990	2000	% change	1990	2000	% change
Accountants	1,488,481	1,762,729	18.4	14.64	22.06	50.7	17.65	25.00	41.7
Doctors	571,320	705,960	23.6	34.10	58.23	70.8	47.91	70.96	48.1
Dentists	155,529	155,715	0.1	24.22	46.66	92.6	48.93	86.90	77.6
Elementary school teachers	3,105,603	3,125,320	0.6	16.28	22.07	35.6	16.50	22.47	36.2
Secondary school teachers	494,326	772,462	56.3	17.14	23.57	37.6	17.50	24.01	37.2
Lawyers	697,272	871,116	24.9	22.97	36.50	58.9	36.95	51.76	40.1
Hairdressers and cosmetologists	661,773	667,365	0.8	5.59	7.79	39.3	8.78	13.08	48.9
U.S. labor force	191,829,270	217,168,077	13.2	11.91	17.53	47.1	13.34	19.35	45.1

SOURCE: Employment and earnings are estimated from the 5% sample of the U.S. Census of Population. Employment estimates are from Scopp (2003, Table 9).

highest levels of income. Wage growth in the U.S. economy was 47.1 percent, and hourly earnings growth was 45.1 percent in nominal values from 1990 to 2000. Table 1.1 presents growth in both wages and earnings. There are substantial bonuses and profit sharing from being involved in private practices in some occupations (e.g., lawyers, physicians, and dentists), and tips and private business revenues are a substantial part of the economic returns for cosmetologists. Growth in hourly wages was 92.6 percent for dentists and more than 70 percent for physicians. It is interesting to observe that the supply of dentists remained constant over the decade, but that the number of doctors increased. Unlike the decline in the number of doctors and their wage growth relative to dentists during the 1930s (Friedman and Kuznets 1945), the hourly earnings of dentists, when profit sharing, dividends, and other income from their practice are taken into account, were higher than they were for physicians by 2000. The relatively lower-wage occupations shown in Table 1.1, like cosmetologists and teachers, saw the smallest wage growth (between 35.6 and 39.3 percent) during the 1990s. However, when hourly earnings are included, which include other business income, cosmetologists' earnings growth was slightly higher than those of accountants. Regulated occupations followed national patterns of growing inequality of earnings by having the highest-wage occupations in 1990 showing the largest wage growth, but lower-wage occupations had smaller wage growth than national averages.

From a public policy perspective, all states have enacted licensing of some occupations. Tabulations by the Council of State Government's affiliated Council on Licensure Enforcement and Regulation (CLEAR) show that more than 800 occupations are licensed in at least one state, but about 50 occupations are licensed in all states (Berry 1986; CLEAR 2004). The path toward licensing usually includes initially becoming either certified or registered, but hardly ever does an occupation move from licensing to certification where others legally can do the work of certified practitioners. The occupation with the largest number of individuals in the profession is public school teachers; from 1984 to 1998, 26 states instituted state exams for entering teaching for the first time. Most state legislatures have hearings during each session dealing with questions of the licensing of occupations. Recently, the Federal Trade Commission (FTC) and the U.S. Justice Department had hearings on the effect of occupational licensing practices on reducing competition on Internet transactions and on competition in health care (Kleiner 2002, 2003). An analysis of income inequality in the United States has shown that being in an occupation—not just educational attainment—is an important determinant of growing relative wage differences among workers (Eckstein and Nagypal 2004). Consequently, barriers to entry into these regulated and high-income occupations, regardless of whether they are licensed, may provide an additional explanation for the growth of income inequality in the United States.

Among universally licensed occupations there are institutional, administrative, and legal factors that are likely to influence entry into an occupation within a state. These are generally perceived to be statutory as well as administrative constraints such as examination requirements that impact labor supply and subsequently earnings (Kleiner 2000). Statutory factors at the state level generally include education for general training, which is defined as years of high school and college education, and occupation-specific years of schooling that include years of professional or trade school. Further measures include specific requirements for good moral character, citizenship, residency in the state for specific periods of time, recommendations from current practitioners, and tests for competency. States can vary in the stringency with which they each set the requirements for practicing in an occupation.

A further set of requirements is established for individuals who attempt to move to the state from elsewhere. These requirements generally include similar general and specific statutory requirements to those entering the occupation but with several notable exceptions, including retaking certain specific parts of the original licensing exam to enter the occupation. Often this also includes working with a licensed practitioner to ensure the out-of-state applicant follows current state procedures. States, however, can establish virtual "treaties" with other states to allow them to accept each other's licensed practitioners without additional education or tests. The statutes and agreements with other political entities vary from accepting any out-of-state applicant who has a valid license at one end of a continuum to acceptance of applicants if they meet the entry requirements in force at the time of initial licensure (Kleiner, Gay, and Greene 1982; Tenn 2001). State entry requirements vary a great deal both across and within occupations in how they allow licensed practitioners from other states or countries to enter and work within their political jurisdictions.

Beyond the statutory factors, each state can establish its own pass rate for entering the occupation even when they use a national standardized test. The pass rate on the same exam can be higher in California than in North Dakota. Individuals considering entering an occupation in a state may decide not to move to a state when the pass rate is low. This reflects the fact that, for most licensed individuals choosing a state in which to locate, initial failure on an exam would result in more study time, lower incomes, and retaking the test.

SOCIAL BENEFITS OF LICENSING

The previous sections have documented the growth and importance of licensing as an institution, but they do not discuss how licensing may impact society. The main benefit usually cited for occupational licensing is improving the quality of services received. Licensing creates greater incentives for individuals to invest in more occupation-specific human capital because they will be able to recoup the full returns on their investment if they do not need to face low-quality substitutes for their services (Akerlof 1970; Shapiro 1986). Under these conditions, some sectors of the market segmented by income or price for the services may benefit more than others, which is what Shapiro calls a "separating equilibrium."

Economists often look at next best solutions that may provide greater choice for both practitioners and consumers. In this case certification may provide many of the same benefits as licensing without the costs of restricting the supply of practitioners or limiting choice for consumers. Licensing is contrasted with certification because, with certification, any person can perform the relevant tasks, but the government or generally another nonprofit agency administers an examination and certifies those who have passed, as well as identifies the level of skill and knowledge for certification. For example, travel agents and car mechanics are among the more than 65 occupations that are generally certified but not licensed (Cox and Foster 1990; Rottenberg 1980). Skeptics of licensing point out that the empirical evidence on the increase in quality, greater training, or avoidance of catastrophes is usually thin or nonexistent. They argue that if a signal of quality is important, certification is a better way of accomplishing the goal than occupational licensing. More-over, many of the skeptics would suggest that any remaining beneficial effects of occupational licensing are more than offset by the monopoly effects of the restriction of supply of practitioners.

QUALITY AND DEMAND EFFECTS OF OCCUPATIONAL REGULATION

The major public policy justification for occupational licensing lies in its role in improving quality of service rendered and, consequently, in generating consumer demand for the service. Licensing is expected to improve quality by setting initial entry requirements in the occupation. These generally include residency requirements, letters from current practitioners regarding good moral character, citizenship, general edu-cation, occupation-specific training levels, and scores on specific tests. States and local governments can also change pass rates to mirror rela-tive supply and demand conditions for the service. For example, when there is perceived to be an oversupply in the occupation, the regulatory board can raise the test scores required to pass the exam thus reducing the number of new entrants (Maurizi 1974; Kleiner 1990).

The consequence of these regulatory practices is a reduction in the flow of entrants into the occupation, which can have several effects on quality. The average quality of service provided increases as less-competent providers of the service are prevented from entering the oc-cupation. Moreover, persons in regulated jobs may think that they can capture additional returns to their occupation-specific training, which may increase the overall competency of the persons in the occupation. However, prices and wages will rise as the result of restricting the num-ber of practitioners, which is expected to reduce quality received by consumers. This would occur as certain low-income consumers would not receive any service due to rising prices. As with any production relationship, other factors such as capital or technology may also con-tribute to the overall quality of service outputs.

Because of these different factors of price and restricting supply of lower-skilled applicants, the effect of regulation on the level of service quality is uncertain. However, changes in technology for service delivery or increases in the amount of capital available may change the impacts of regulation on outcomes. It is impossible on theoretical grounds to determine whether more intense regulation will increase or decrease the quality of the service provided.

The countervailing forces of the effect of occupational licensing on quality carry over into the ambiguity about the effect of licensing on the quantity of the service demanded. The assumption is that the higher price should discourage consumption of the service. However, higher (or less-variable) quality may lead to an increased demand for the service by consumers. Moreover, one additional question is whether all consumers benefit from this increase in quality or if there are also distributional impacts as well.

Developing empirical evidence on these issues of quality and demand is difficult. Typically, direct observations or estimates of the quality of a service (e.g., the quality of a dental visit) are not available. For many licensed occupations, like barbers and cosmetologists, it is not clear how one would measure quality. Perhaps measures of outputs such as customer satisfaction, complaints to state licensing boards, or liability insurance rates may serve as adequate proxies.

An alternative approach is to examine the "productivity effects of licensing" by examining actual outputs (Carroll and Gaston 1981). For dentistry, Kleiner and Kudrle (2000) examined the records of U.S. Air Force recruits who were from different states and for whom there were individual records over their lifetimes. They found little statistical support for the role of tougher licensing measured either through characteristics of state licensing statutes or through pass rates on measures of dental health. Further examinations of the impact of occupational regulation on malpractice insurance rates or complaints to state licensing boards also found few effects of tougher regulations. However, they did find a positive impact of licensing on the prices of some dental services as well as on the hourly earnings of dentists.

LICENSING OCCUPATIONS AND LABOR SUPPLY

The dominant view among economists is that occupational licensing restricts the supply of labor to the occupation and thereby drives up the price of labor and of services rendered (Rottenberg 1980). State-regulated occupations can use political institutions such as state legislatures or city councils to control initial entry and in-migration, thereby restricting supply and raising the wages of licensed practitioners. There is assumed to be a "once and for all" income gain that accrues to current members of the occupation who are "grandparented" in and do not have to meet the newly established standard (Perloff 1980). Individuals who attempt to enter the occupation in the future will need to balance the economic rents of the field's increased monopoly power against the greater difficulty of meeting the entrance requirements.

Once an occupation is regulated, members of that occupation in a geographic or political jurisdiction can implement tougher statutes or examination pass rates and may achieve an economic gain relative to those who have easier requirements by further restricting the supply of labor and obtaining economic rents for incumbents (Kleiner 1990). Restrictions could include lowering the pass rate on licensing exams, imposing higher general and specific requirements, and implementing tougher residency requirements that limit new arrivals in the area from qualifying for a license. Moreover, individuals who have finished schooling in the occupation may decide not to go to a particular political jurisdiction where the pass rate is low because both the economic and shame costs may be high (Kandel and Lazear 1992). Of course, an individual who takes a test in Mississippi may have different qualifications and abilities than someone in California. Consequently, any analysis of pass-rate effects needs to be tempered with some controls for the academic quality of the test takers both across states and over time. One additional effect of licensing is that individuals who are not allowed to practice in an occupation as a consequence of regulation may then enter an unlicensed occupation, shifting the supply curve outward and driving down wages in these unregulated occupations.

The costs of failing an exam required by the state can be quite high. For example, the present value cost of failing the exam in dentistry is estimated to be about $54,000 in 1997 dollars when reduced earnings growth, lost experience, and nominal earnings growth differences are accounted for over time (Kleiner and Kudrle 2000). Long residency requirements or the necessity of retaking new state-specific parts of a licensing exam further impede geographic mobility across states or local jurisdictions (Kleiner, Gay, and Greene 1982). For example, states like Florida, Arizona, Hawaii, and California have traditionally had longer continuous residency requirements for many regulated occupations, presumably to keep persons from states with more inclement weather during winter months from moving to the state and working in the occupation. Other states focus on unique parts of an occupation, such as the "gold foil" method of filling teeth, which was used in California and was only examined within that state's licensing exam. Out-of-state applicants were required to learn this unique procedure to pass the California exam.

ARE THERE LICENSING WAGE AND PRICE PREMIUMS?

The analysis provided in this book will examine wage premiums as a consequence of licensing by focusing on two questions. First, do licensed occupations have higher earnings as a consequence of government regulations in comparison to other similar unregulated occupations? Second, when changes occur among licensed occupations, do they have labor market consequences?

To examine the first question of whether there is a wage gap for licensed occupations, I estimate how much regulated workers would make if they were not regulated. This methodology entails holding constant human capital characteristics such as education and experience to determine whether individuals in licensed occupations are more likely to have higher earnings than persons in unlicensed occupations. This approach assumes that the earnings difference is attributable to licensing and that there is not much spillover from the licensed to the unlicensed occupations. Also, individuals with greater unobserved ability may choose to enter a licensed occupation where the economic returns are greater, rather than occupations that require similar aptitude but are unregulated. Given the large queue of persons wishing to enter these regulated occupations, part of the returns to licensed occupations may be the higher-quality labor market abilities of persons in regulated occupations, which consumers in turn see as raising the quality of service in these areas.

Economists generally accept that licensing is a way of limiting competition since they argue that licenses limit labor supply, often quite explicitly through varying the pass rates and statutory regulations on residency requirements. As a result of this restriction in labor supply, prices and wages rise. For example, the number of dentists has declined and their earnings relative to doctors has risen. Moreover, economists have often argued that certification, such as granting degrees in the area of expertise, could easily assure minimum quality with less impact on supply.

COMPARING UNIONS AND LICENSING

Figure 1.1 shows the trends in both union and licensing coverage from 1950 through the early 2000s. Whereas union membership and coverage has declined from the mid-1950s from almost 35 percent to 12.5 percent, the opposite is true for the coverage of occupational licensing, which has gone from about 4.5 percent in the 1950s to more than 20 percent after 2000. Nevertheless, when an occupation becomes regulated, there are some similarities to union limitations on entry at the firm level (Freeman and Medoff 1984). Where management agrees to a union shop provision as part of a collective bargaining agreement, generally only members of the union can be employed at that workplace to do certain tasks. This presumably increases the economic leverage of the union and also may contribute to the more than 20 percent premium received by the average union member (Blanchflower and Bryson 2003). Unions in newly organized establishments introduce voice benefits such as grievance procedures to the organization and a standardization of work practices. However, recent evidence on the union effects shortly following an organizing drive shows that unions have a modest effect on wages in newly organized establishments, and the same lack of a large increase in earnings initially also may be true of persons in licensed occupations (Freeman and Kleiner 1990). Many of the estimates presented in this book examine whether changes in licensing statutes and administrative procedures impacted changes in labor market conditions (such as wages, employment, and quality) in the period from 1990 to 2000.

However, a major difference between occupational licensing and unions is that licensing may be a more secure job classification. It is rare

Figure 1.1 Comparisons in the Trends of Labor Market Institutions: Licensing and Unionization

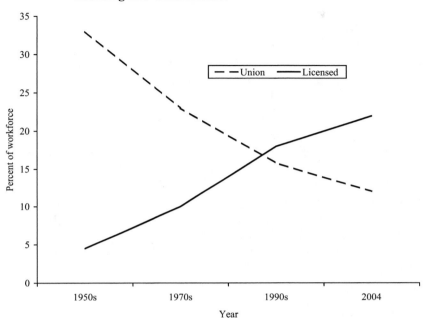

NOTE: Tabulations for licensing coverage for the 1950s are from Council of State Governments (1952), which lists licensed occupations in the public use census sample for 1950. For the 1960s, the tabulations are from Greene (1969), which links the available listing of licensed occupations to census tabulations. The data for the 1980s are from Kleiner (1990) tabulations, and new estimates were developed for 2000. Estimates for union density are from the Bureau of Labor Statistics (1979) and Hirsch and Macpherson (2005).

for an occupation to become deregulated by a government agency, for the regulatory powers of a licensing board to be stripped by the legislature, or for the licensing board to ask to be terminated. There is one rare example: the occupational licensing of watchmakers was eliminated in Minnesota when the number of persons in the occupation in the state dropped to less than 100 individuals. In contrast, unions can be and are decertified as representatives of employees under National Labor Relations Board election procedures. Annually, hundreds of decertification elections are conducted in the private sector, and unions lose more than half of these elections (Fossum 2002).

FOCUS OF THE BOOK

During the 1990s there were many changes in the licensing provisions among U.S. states, and the pass rates for entry into the occupations changed substantially. Did these changes have any impact on the earnings and employment growth of these already regulated occupations? This book will examine changes in employment regulation in the occupations that increased regulation relative to ones that experienced little change.

The remainder of this book is organized as follows. Chapter 2 examines the development of licensing as a labor market institution. Chapter 3 focuses on the quality impacts of occupational licensing, with an emphasis on the influence of these benefits on the demand for licensing and its effects on price. Chapter 4 analyzes the effects of licensing on the earnings of regulated occupations relative to unregulated ones, with special attention to accountants, cosmetologists, dentists, lawyers, and teachers in the United States. Chapter 5 shows the trends in the statutes and administrative procedures by state and develops estimates of the economic costs of licensing to the economy. Chapter 6 expands the analysis for regulated occupations to the three largest nations in the EU, namely France, Germany, and the UK. The concluding chapter presents rationale for standardization of licensed services, analyzes the employment growth impacts of occupational licensing, summarizes the major empirical findings of the book, and develops policy alternatives and implications of occupational licensing as an emerging labor market institution.

Notes

1. Dentists, doctors, and lawyers are licensed in every state, fortune tellers are licensed in Maryland, and frog farmers are licensed in South Dakota (Hollings and Pike-Nase 1997; Studenmund 1997).
2. The methods used to calculate the percentage of the workforce in licensed occupations involved using the listing of licensed occupations from the Department of Labor's Labor Market Information Survey and matching it with occupations in the 2000 census. If no match was obtained, the occupation was dropped. The number working in the licensed occupation in each state was estimated from the census and used to calculate a weighted average of the percentage of the U.S.

workforce that works in a licensed occupation. Given the growth in employment in service industries, where the licensing of occupations is greatest, the vast majority of the employment growth in licensed occupations occurred in already-regulated employment during the late 1990s through the early part of the 2000s. Estimates from Minnesota show that three-fourths of the employment growth occurred in already-licensed occupations (Broat et al. 2004).

2
Development of Occupational Licensing as a Labor Market Institution

The modern state owes and attempts to perform a duty to protect the public from those who seek for one purpose or another to obtain money. When one does so through the practice of a calling, the state may have an interest in shielding the public against the untrustworthy, the incompetent, or the irresponsible.

> —Robert H. Jackson, U.S. Supreme Court Justice 1941–1954, U.S Attorney General 1940–1941, and American Chief of Counsel, War Trials at Nuremberg 1945, in *Thomas v. Collins* (1945).

The overthrow of the medieval guild system was an indispensable early step in the rise of freedom in the Western world. It was a sign of the triumph of liberal ideas, and widely recognized as such, that by the mid-nineteenth century, in Britain, the United States, and to a lesser extent on the continent of Europe, men could pursue whatever trade or occupation they wished without the by-your-leave of any governmental or quasi-governmental authority. In more recent decades, there has been a retrogression, an increasing tendency for particular occupations to be restricted to individuals licensed to practice them by the state.

> —Milton Friedman, Nobel Laureate Economist, in *Capitalism and Freedom* (1962a, p. 137).

As these two statements suggest, there are often conflicting views of the goals and outcomes achieved by occupational licensing. This chapter aims to provide the institutional setting for the theoretical and empirical analysis that follows, building a background for the development of this labor market institution. The background begins with the origins of occupational licensing, with an emphasis on its development in Europe and the United States. Following that, I review several studies that show the benefits of licensing during the early part of the twentieth century. The results of these studies suggest that initially the public may benefit from more regulation as quality increases, but long-term effects of licensing are more likely to be dominated by restricted competition due to the more strict entrance requirements into the profession. Moreover, the growth of information technology through the Internet minimizes the argument that licensing reduces asymmetry of information between consumers and suppliers of the service (Kleiner 2002). Further on, I outline the major court cases and their decisions that made licensing by states part of the legal framework in the United States. Finally, I look at a case study of one particular state, which details recent trends in occupational licensing for the state of Minnesota, with some comparisons to its neighboring state of Wisconsin. This case study shows evidence of the extent to which the legislature and licensing boards act to both protect the public and how they could be "captured" by the members of the occupation.

The regulation of occupations in the United States and other nations takes various forms. The three major forms of occupational regulation are licensing, certification, and registration. The Council of State Governments in the United States established a special agency to focus exclusively on occupational licensing. That agency is the Council on Licensure, Enforcement, and Regulation (CLEAR), and its stated objective is to improve "the quality and understanding of regulation in order to enhance public protection" (CLEAR 2004). The council also developed widely accepted national definitions for each of the categories of occupational regulation. The toughest form of regulation is licensure, and CLEAR refers to this as the right-to-practice. Under licensure laws, it is illegal for a person to practice a profession without first meeting state standards. A less-restrictive form of regulation is certification, where states grant title (occupational right-to-title) protection to persons meeting predetermined standards. Those without certification may perform the duties of the occupation, but they may not use the title. The least restrictive form of regulation is registration, which usually requires individuals to file their names, addresses, and qualifications with a government agency before practicing the occupation. This may include posting a bond or paying a fee to have the practitioner's name listed by the state among those in the occupation. The regulation of occupations in the United States and other nations falls under the continuum of little to highly restrictive forms of government regulation of occupations.

DEVELOPMENT OF OCCUPATIONAL REGULATION

Occupational licensing has a long and prominent history as a labor market institution.[1] The Babylonian Code of Hammurabi (c. 1780 BCE) stipulated both the fees patients were to pay for medical services and the punishments for negligent treatment. Women were barred from medical practice in Greece during the period around 300 BCE, and examining and licensing boards existed for "healers" in Baghdad in 931 CE (Gross 1984). Even the Hippocratic Oath taken by Greek physicians as early as the fourth century BCE, urging physicians to do no harm, also provided provisions regarding conflict of interest and the need to refrain from wrongdoing and corruption. In the Middle Ages in Europe during the course of the Holy Roman Empire, physicians were required to have specific years of schooling, and those who did not have the appropriate qualifications had their property confiscated and the sentence of a year in prison (Gross 1984).

The merchant guilds that developed during the Middle Ages and "Enlightenment" in Europe later served as models for current professional associations. The guilds limited entry into occupations and enforced requirements that merchants only hire from the guild. Both the university and the guilds tied education to licensing, also serving to tie the state to the professions. As educational historian H.G. Carman states:

> The medieval universities both trained and licensed. In reality a degree was a certificate of competence which in the cases of law and medicine usually conveyed certain exclusive rights of practice to its holder. Similarly, the guilds which evolved into professional bodies often gave training and always attempted to give exclusive rights of practice to their members. (Carman 1958, p. 269)

In 1518 in England, Henry VIII established the Royal College of Physicians and Surgeons, which gave the state and the church the power to license physicians. Through much of Europe during this period, another licensing requirement was membership in the proper church (Gross 1984).

The development of occupational licensing in the United States borrowed much from the European experience. The first physician licensing occurred in the new British colony of Virginia in 1639. By 1800 13 of the 16 states had given the authority to examine and license to the state medical authorities. By 1840 there were 30 medical schools in the United States and 77 by 1876. Medical education varied from a few months to two years (Tabachinik 1976). However, almost anyone could claim to be a doctor during this period, but there is little evidence that the trained or "regular" doctors during this period did much better than the unlicensed doctors in terms of patient outcomes (Ehrenreich and English 1973). In contrast to the earlier period at the time of the U.S. Civil War, the early licensing system had fallen away and there was still no effective occupational licensing system in place (Council of State Governments 1952).

In the latter half of the nineteenth century, modern professional and scientific associations were formed, including one for physicians in 1847, pharmacists in 1852, and lawyers in 1877. One of the major methods of obtaining integrity for these organizations was to obtain state sanction for these occupations and the individuals in them (Carman 1958). The first modern medical practice legislation was passed in Texas in 1873. By 1905, 39 states were licensing physicians. Similarly nurses formed a national association in 1896, and 40 states were licensing nurses by 1926 (Gross 1984).

The major period during which licensing laws initially were passed was 1890 to 1910. In his article on "Freedom of Contract," Law Professor Lawrence Friedman relates the major legal principles on licensing and other labor reforms that were taking place during this period (Friedman 1965):

> In the same period 1890 to 1910, occupational licensing first achieved a firm foothold in the statute-books of most American states. Laws to license doctors, plumbers, barbers, funeral directors, nurses, electricians, horse shoers, dentists, and the practitioners of many other occupations were debated, propounded and very often passed. Many of these laws gave rise to constitutional test cases. Unlike the more spectacular labor law cases, the licensing cases called down no pronouncements of doom and enlisted neither pro-

ponents nor opponents in high and academic places to argue validity and propriety on the basis of first principles. This was a quieter,
blander area of constitutional law. From the standpoint of logic
and of life, however, the cases involved first principles no less than
those which arose under wage and hour laws. If a workman had a
constitutional and God-given right to work eleven hours a day in
a bakeshop, or to be paid in kind instead of cash, he should have
had a similar right to contract with an unlicensed barber or to buy
a laxative from a druggist without a certificate on his wall.

The major Supreme Court case that established the right of states
to grant licenses was *Dent v. West Virginia* (1888). The decision established the state law purporting to protect the health, welfare, or safety of
citizens and was justified as having a rational relationship to the legiti-
mate end of government under the police power banner (Gross 1984).
This decision took away the federal right of preemption in the arena of
occupational licensing and gave it to the states. This is different from
most other later labor laws, such as the National Labor Relations Act,
which established federal law over any state provisions dealing with the
regulation of unions and management on collective bargaining. Occupational regulation continued to grow and, by 1889, 10 additional occupations besides law and medicine were licensed. A steady increase saw
30 occupations licensed in 1920, including more than 2,800 statutory
provisions in the different states (Greene 1969). Following World War
II, the number of regulated occupations continued to expand as more
occupations became well-organized and sought licensing from state
governments (Council of State Governments 1952). In 2003 the Council of State Governments estimated that more than 800 occupations are
licensed in at least one state and more than 1,100 are either licensed,
certified, or registered (Brinegar and Schmitt 1992; Smith-Peters and
Smith-Peters 2004). Although the vast majority of occupations have
sought licensing through their associations from federal, state, county,
or city sources, there are instances of occupations for which licensing
was imposed mainly as a result of perceived corruption. For example,
stockbrokers were brought under federal regulation in response to the
financial scandals that grew out of the crash of the stock market in 1929
(Gellhorn 1976).

QUALITY FIRST, THEN RESTRICTIONS ON COMPETITION?

The initial work on estimating the impacts of licensing focused on the ability of the occupations to restrict the supply of new entrants into the occupation. The classic work by the future Nobel Laureates Milton Friedman and Simon Kuznets analyzed the differences in the regulatory restrictions of doctors and dentists from 1900 to the early 1940s. Based in large part on the greater ability of doctors to restrict entry through their professional associations by eliminating "overcrowding" in the profession relative to dentists, the authors attribute about half of the 23 percent difference in the earnings within the two professions to these restrictions on supply (Friedman and Kuznets 1945). On the other hand, they do not attempt to examine the impact of occupational regulation on the quality of the service. Rather, the focus of the discussion in their book is on the restrictions on competition during the period of initial licensure of many of the major regulated occupations in the United States.

One of the major issues on costs and benefits of occupational licensing is that, initially, licensing is a product of consumer demands for higher levels of credible information on the quality of service. Law and Kim (2004) state that from 1880 to 1930, licensing laws were passed in response to the growth of knowledge within the professions and the reduction in transportation costs that made urbanization more feasible. In fact they find that urbanization and population density were the dominant factors in the passage of initial licensing laws during the twentieth century. They argue that there is evidence of information asymmetry as the major force for regulation as individuals move to an urban area and have limited information on the quality of key service providers such as lawyers and doctors. A similar argument can be made currently for the maintenance of licensing laws as immigrants, the poor, and the elderly also have little knowledge of physicians' or attorneys' competence or have little experience with information sources like the Internet or other sources of data on service quality. Consequently, licensing offers a relatively low-cost method of providing information on critical services.

Law and Kim (2004), however, find that licensing has an impact on restrictions in the growth rate in employment for certain key occupations such as dentists, physicians, and cosmetologists. They are unable to find any impact of their licensing index on the incomes of physicians. However, during the early part of the twentieth century, as Friedman and Kuznets (1945) point out, the mechanism through which physicians restricted supply was through limiting the number of positions in medical schools and only tangentially through the passage of tougher licensing exams. One important finding from the licensing of physicians was the increase in malpractice lawsuits following the regulation of physicians. This may be a consequence of higher consumer expectations from regulation. When an occupation becomes licensed, the licensing results in the creation of regulatory boards and greater visibility for the occupation, an expectation of higher-quality services, and an infrastructure that allows lawsuits and other forms of consumer voice to be heard relative to a regime of no licensing. The greater visibility provided to members of the licensed occupation may counterbalance any greater quality benefits of regulation through measures such as complaints or malpractice insurance rates.

From Law and Kim's (2004) analysis there appears to be many similarities between the workings of the regulation of occupations and those of another labor market institution, unionization. For example, Freeman and Kleiner (1990) find that initially unions bring to an establishment voice benefits such as a grievance procedure, the posting of job requirements for promotion, and seniority-based layoffs and recalls, but there are few initial wage and benefit increases. Only after the union is established are the employees and their union leadership willing to go after wages and benefits. These "monopoly effects" have led to a union wage premium of 10 to 25 percent over time (Freeman and Medoff 1984). In a similar manner, licensing and unions initially provide nonwage benefits of perceived quality of working conditions and later seek outcomes that result in increases in earnings or greater control of who works and under what conditions. During the period of initial regulation from 1880 to 1930, occupational licensing provided a form of information to consumers on minimum quality (Law and Kim 2004). As basic science grew in the health occupations, the migration from rural to urban areas became substantial and immigrants were a large percentage of the urban landscape, occupational licensing provided basic information on essential services for newcomers. Although licensing provided some information on quality, it did so with the cost

of higher prices and slower growth in employment of the service occupations that it regulated.

LEGAL BASIS OF STATE OCCUPATIONAL LICENSING

As mentioned earlier, the *Dent v. West Virginia* decision in 1888
gave the first federal justification to the states to have the power to regulate occupational licensing. In another major court decision, *Parker v.
Brown* (1943), the Supreme Court held that antitrust statutes are aimed
at private, not state, action and ruled that a California statute constrict-
ing competitive marketing in the private sector was legal (Gellhorn
1976). The implication of the law as stated in this case was that a state
must command, not merely permit, a restraint of trade in order to immu-
nize it against federal antitrust laws. This case also gave the states wide
latitude in setting occupational licensing laws without the oversight of
the federal courts.

Perhaps the most important case dealing with licensing practices
was decided by the Supreme Court in *Goldfarb v. Virginia* (1975). The
Court ruled that the state bar's policy of an association's minimum fee
schedule violated the Sherman Act's prohibition of combinations in restraint of trade. This case vindicated lawyers' abilities to advertise and
charge fees that can be negotiated with the client and not set by the
bar association or the state (Gellhorn 1976). Prior to this case, many
state and federal courts thought that the "learned professions" should be
treated differently because their goal was to provide services necessary
to the community rather than to generate "profits." Consequently, their
activities did not fall within the terms "trade and commerce" in Section
One of the Sherman Act. The central finding of the Supreme Court in
the Goldfarb case was that professional activities have a sufficient effect on interstate commerce to support the Sherman Act jurisdiction.

In subsequent decades, both the FTC and the Antitrust Division of
the Department of Justice have undertaken a broad enforcement program
designed to eliminate private restrictions on business practices of state-
licensed professions that may adversely impact the competitive process
and raise the prices or decrease the quality of professional services.
From 1976 to 1978 the FTC had more than doubled its expenditure

on funds it allocated to occupational licensing research and litigation (Clarkson and Muris 1980). For example, since the *Goldfarb v. Virginia* decision, these two federal agencies have sued or charged the American Medical Association, the American Institute of Certified Public Accountants, the California Dental Association, the National Society of Professional Engineers, and other public or quasi-public associations in order to alleviate restrictions on advertising, minimum fee agreements, restrictions on competitive bidding, and increases in requirements for entering a profession (Committee on Competition Law and Policy 2000).

Recent issues involve the attempts by the professions to capture work from other occupations or to restrict the ability of licensed or unlicensed occupations, such as alternative health care providers, to do work within the occupations' "span of control." For example, in South Carolina, the state dental association (through the state legislature) required dentists to examine Medicaid-eligible children rather than allow them to be seen only by dental hygienists (Nash 2003). The FTC perceived this as a restraint of trade problem that raised the cost to the federal government of funding the Medicaid program for eligible young children. These U.S. policies to enhance competition have resulted in more price and marketing competition within and across occupations following individuals entering into the occupation in comparison to other nations in the Organisation for Economic Co-operation and Development (OECD), which consists of the major economically developed countries (Garoupa 2004).

Since the *Goldfarb v. Virginia* decision, professional associations have been more modest in attempting to lobby states to become licensed, and states have opened up the occupations' work practices to advertising and less-restrictive marketing practices. Nevertheless, the number of licensed occupations has continued to grow, but at a slower pace, because it is rare for an occupation to move toward a less or unregulated status once it has become regulated. The growth in employment in service industries during the past decade has resulted in a growth in employment in licensed occupations as well. In fact, during the past decade, most of the growth of employment in licensed occupations has occurred as a consequence of employment growth within occupations rather than increases in the number of newly regulated occupations.

In order to illustrate how licensing works in greater depth, I use one state to provide more detailed information for that state's licensing provisions and practices. I chose to examine Minnesota, a state that has been at the forefront of the "good government" movement and has attempted to provide clear guidelines for new occupations seeking to become regulated. Examining this state in depth, with access to more detailed information on the institution of licensing, will also allow the subsequent analysis of the United States and Western Europe in the context of the detailed issues raised within these case studies.

HOW LICENSING WORKS: A CASE STUDY OF MINNESOTA

Although a broader examination of state-by-state regulation of occupations is instructive, much can be learned about how licensing works by examining a single state in detail. As a result of the evolution of the legal system in the United States, most licensing takes place at the state level. For this analysis, I chose Minnesota since it is a state with an emphasis on "good government," and it has evolved its regulatory policy from little oversight by the legislature to establishing clear criteria for licensing and tougher regulations for occupations. This section also develops comparisons of the impact of licensing versus certification on the complaints of consumers for certain regulated occupations in Wisconsin and Minnesota. Moreover, Minnesota has gathered considerable data on licensing and devoted much effort to reports from the state's legislative auditor on this subject (Broat et al. 2004; Office of the Legislative Auditor, State of Minnesota 1999).

Occupational regulation began in the state in the 1880s, starting with physicians (1883), dentists (1885), and accountants (1909) (Council of State Governments 1952). These initial dates of licensure were similar to other states in the Midwest, but they were earlier than most other states nationally. There was a steady increase in the number of occupations seeking to become regulated. For example, 20 occupations were regulated in Minnesota in 1950, a number that included about 5 percent of the workforce (Council of State Governments 1952). During the 1960s and 1970s, the state, along with many others, received several requests annually, mainly from organized representatives of the occupations seeking licensure (Kleiner and Gordon 1996). Although there were some changes in census categories over time, making exact matches somewhat imprecise, the number of occupations regulated rose from 47 to 141 in the period from 1968 to 1990 (Kleiner and Gordon 1996). From 1998 to 2004, the percentage of persons in licensed occupations grew by about 1 percent, or approximately 100,000 workers. About 75 percent of overall growth was in employment in already licensed occupations, and about 25 percent (approximately 25,000 workers) of overall employment increases was due to the addition of individuals in newly licensed occupations (Broat et al. 2004). This increase is largely a result of the growth in the service and health-related industry employment during this period. In 2004 the state regulated a total of 167 occupations, of which 131 are licensed with their own boards, 19 are certified, 15 are registered, and two are regulated via the "after credentialing" activity of the occupation, which is a weaker form of registration (Broat et al. 2004).[2] The percentage of workers in occupations regulated by the state in 2004, using state of Minnesota internal measures of regulation, was approximately 30.2 percent of the total state workforce. Approximately 27 percent were licensed, 2 percent were certified, and 1 percent were registered (Broat et al. 2004).[3] In comparison to other states, Minnesota ranks in the middle tier of states in both the number of occupations regulated and percentage of the workforce licensed.

Table 2.1 shows changes in occupational regulation in Minnesota from 1999 to 2004, the period of the last two reports to the Minnesota State Auditor on occupational licensing (Office of the Legislative Auditor, State of Minnesota 1999). As the table shows, the trend in Minnesota is toward regulating more occupations or increasing the level of regulation for existing occupations. For example, midwives and multipurpose water piping system contractor/installers became licensed. Physical therapists and occupational therapists moved from being certified to being licensed. Other occupations lost their own independent board and were merged into larger commercial or medical licensing boards. One of these occupations was weather modifiers. Watchmakers were deregulated because their numbers diminished to just a few. In general, the trend has been toward more regulation through the licensing of new occupations and increasing the toughness of regulation for certified occupations by requiring them to license their work. The goal of most of the occupational associations seeking regulation in Minnesota is licensing rather than certification or registration because it gives

Table 2.1 Changes in Occupational Regulation in Minnesota, 1999–2004

Newly licensed occupations	Newly regulated occupations	Occupations with stricter regulation	Regulated occupations merged with other licensing boards
Licensed professional counselor (LPC) (2003)	Unlicensed complementary and alternative health care practitioners (2000)	Physical therapists (certified to licensed – 1999)	Weather modifier (1999)
Traditional midwife (1999)	Athlete agents (registered – 2002)	Occupational therapist (certified to licensed – 2000)	
Commercial animal waste technician (2000)	Environmental health food manager (certified – 1999)		
Power limited technician (2002)			
Multi-purpose water piping system contractor/installer (2003)			

SOURCE: Broat et al. (2004).

the occupation control of the standards and the work. No occupations went from licensing to certification during this period.

GOALS AND EFFORT OF REGULATORY BOARDS

The goals of regulatory boards are to control entry into the occupation and to enforce the standards of practice among licensed practitioners. Typically, board administrators examine the credentials of applicants and determine whether their education, experience, and "ethical" fitness meet statutory or administrative admission requirements. They often decide whether certain schools meet the requisite training standards in the occupation. This generally involves setting an approved list of schools that meet the minimum standards for the occupation. A board may contract out the examinations for passing the licensing exam, but it will often set the pass rate for the examination. Boards are also required to administer the reciprocity or endorsement provisions between the states to determine who qualifies to be regulated within the state if they were initially in a regulated occupation elsewhere. They set standards for persons who have licenses from other countries. Boards generally have the authority to investigate violations of standards and conduct hearings when there is evidence of violations of state standards and if a revocation of a license is warranted. Finally, they collect annual fees and can levy any fines. Often revenues collected from licensed practitioners become part of the general state budget.

The way regulatory boards operate is not uniform. Many of the licensing boards meet often to discuss issues of quality and disciplinary procedures. Often new approaches to setting standards in the occupation and the ways that information can be disseminated are discussed. Subcommittees usually meet to discuss the cut-off scores for passing the state licensing exam. Economist Milton Friedman (1962a) states that boards limit new entrants so that current licensees will not be compelled to charge higher prices or engage in unethical practices to generate more clients in order to make an "acceptable income." Other issues considered are the criteria for accepting out-of-state applicants and foreign nationals.

The time allocated to meetings varies a great deal. Table 2.2 gives the variations in the time allocated to meeting annually in Minnesota by regulated occupation. For example, "peace officers" spend less than 1 hour per month on board-related activities, whereas the board dealing with the licensing of public school teachers spends about 10 hours per month on licensing-related issues (Broat et al. 2004). There does not appear to be a relationship between the number of persons in an occupation and time spent on licensing-related activities. For example, barbers have only 2,700 licensed practitioners, but licensing board members spend more than 8 hours per month on regulatory meetings in 2003. Conversely, the licensing board that regulates electricians and related fields with more than 27,800 practitioners spends about one-fifth as much time in meetings as other licensed occupations presented in Table 2.2 (e.g., barbers in 2003). The allocation of time for licensing-related activities by board members varies a great deal, suggesting that the impacts on labor market outcomes may also vary by state and occupation, depending on whether the board is focused on the quality or supply aspects of occupational regulation.

Table 2.2 Average Total Number of Hours Spent by Board Members in Meetings and on Other Board Activities in Minnesota

Board title	FY 2003	FY 2004
Board of Peace Officer Training and Standards	7.6	10.1
Board of Electricity	18.5	22.4
Board of Teaching	91.2	115.3
Board of Barber Examiners	104.3	61.8
Board of Accountancy	68.8	94.2
Board of Architecture, Engineering, Land Surveying, Landscape Architecture, Geoscience, and Interior Design	100.7	101.5

SOURCE: Broat et al. (2004).

HOW DO OCCUPATIONS BECOME LICENSED?

In Minnesota, as in many other states that regulate occupations through the legislative process, licensing appears to be responsive to political pressure from occupational associations seeking to become regulated. Occupations that are well-organized and have well-funded campaigns with no organized opposition are more likely to find themselves at the top of the agenda before occupational regulatory commissions. This is consistent with other evidence from Illinois, which showed that occupations whose practitioners work for individual consumers (e.g., barbers) have an easier time getting licensed than do, for example, electricians who were opposed in Illinois by groups such as farmers when they attempted to become regulated (Wheelan 2005). Minnesota passed legislation in 1976 that established criteria for the passage of new licensing laws (Office of the Legislative Auditor, State of Minnesota 1999). This provision, Chapter 214, establishes the criteria for assessing any proposed licensing law (Office of the Legislative Auditor, State of Minnesota 1999). The criteria stated in detail in Appendix Table A.1 are the questions that all legislators on the regulatory commission are required to consider and document when an occupation seeks to become regulated. The central questions focus on both quality and restriction of supply issues that form the essence of issues on occupational licensing. Beyond the forms that the legislators are required to complete, the advocates from the occupations who want to become licensed are also required to complete a form providing evidence supporting their position that the legislature should pass a bill regulating the occupation (see Appendix Table A.2). In both cases the burden of proof is on the occupation to provide a compelling reason for the job to be regulated.

Although this is the policy for the legislature, the practice is often quite different. The surveys are often not completed, and blank copies exist in the minutes (Minnesota Legislature, Senate 2000, 2002). Even though it is a policy for associations representing occupational groups to address the issues raised in the memo, only two groups addressed the memos during a recent legislative session: traditional midwives and massage therapists, and oriental bodywork therapists (Minnesota Legislature, Senate 2000, 2002). Of these two bills, only the midwives legislation was passed (Minnesota Legislature, Senate 2000). During the following legislative session in 2001–2002, the same trends concerning the practice of not completing the proper evaluation of occupational regulation continued. There were a number of bills that went before the Legislature. All except one bill were tabled in a joint subcommittee. There is little detailed public record of these meetings (Minnesota Legislature, Senate 2002). The one occupation that made it through these hearings, dental assistants, was not passed into law (Minnesota Legislature, Senate 2002).

Nevertheless, establishing criteria for the regulation of occupations in the state appears to have had some effect on the composition of new legislation. Table 2.3 shows the proposed and adopted bills on occupational regulation for the period from 1981 through 2003. For example, from 1981 through 1998, a third of the bills proposed attempted to license new occupations, and 29 percent of them passed. Following the tighter implementation of the criteria for evaluating new licensing laws during the 1999–2003 sessions, only 26 percent of the bills proposed involved licensing a new occupation and 74 percent involved modifying an existing occupation. This shift implies that a trend exists toward making entry provisions more difficult or adding continuing education requirements (Broat et al. 2004).

Table 2.4 gives the number and percentage of bills that were proposed at the Minnesota legislature on occupational regulation, by industry, from 1995 to 2003. The last column in the table also shows the percentage of the Minnesota workforce for each of the industries covered. The numbers of bills proposed that deal with occupational regulation in the state by the regulated sectors are substantially higher than their percentage in the Minnesota workforce. The data are divided into the periods before and after the implementation of the tougher enforcement of Chapter 214 and the report of the legislative auditor in 1999 on occupational regulation. The basic data show that the majority of bills on occupational regulation were in the health sector, with 53 percent of all proposed legislation from 1995 to 1998 focused on this sector, and more than 67 percent of all legislation from 1999 through 2003 was focused on the regulation of health occupations.

To complement the information in Table 2.4, Table 2.5 presents financial contributions to the Minnesota legislatures' leadership by industry sectors that have interests in occupational regulation.[4] Consistent

Table 2.3 Composition of Proposed Legislation on Occupational Licensing in Minnesota, 1981–2003[a]

Type	1981–1998			1999–2003		
	Bills proposed	Bills passed	% of bills passed	Bills proposed	Bills passed	% of bills passed
Modifying existing law	158	76	48	64	32	50
New occupations regulated	79	23	29	22	7	32
Total proposed and passed	237	99	42	86	39	45

[a] In 1999 new criteria were adopted for legislators to follow when occupations requested regulation.
SOURCE: Adapted from Broat et al. (2004).

Table 2.4 Bills Proposed by the Minnesota Legislature on Occupational Regulation, by Industry, 1995–2003

	1995–1998	% of total bills	1999–2003	% of total bills	% of total employment in Minnesota in 2003
Accounting	5	7.58	5	5.81	0.6
Construction	4	6.06	4	4.65	4.6
Education	7	10.61	0	0.00	2.9
Health	35	53.03	58	67.44	12.2
Mental health	8	12.12	9	10.47	—[a]
Public safety	0	0.00	0	0.00	12.2
Social work	3	4.55	0	0.00	1.9
Other regulated	4	6.06	10	11.63	4.4
Total	66		86		38.8

[a] Mental health employment was subsumed under the general health category.
SOURCE: Adapted from Broat et al. (2004).

Table 2.5 Total Donations by Major Sectors to the Leadership of Each House of the Minnesota Legislature Relative to Employment, 1996–2004

	House ($)	Senate ($)	Total ($)	% of total lobbying expenditures	% of total employment in Minnesota in 2003
Accounting	2,004	6,497	8,501	2	0.6
Construction	17,767	31,085	48,852	11	4.6
Education	32,002	39,403	71,405	15	2.9
Health	59,921	75,734	135,655	29	12.2
Public safety	70,109	45,619	115,728	25	12.2
Other	33,846	47,905	81,751	18	4.4
Total	216,060	246,859	462,919	100	36.9

NOTE: All amounts are in 2004 dollars. Mental health was subsumed under the general health category.
SOURCE: Adapted from Broat et al. (2004).

with a "capture theory" approach to the impact of regulation, which states that those who are regulated attempt to monopolize the process, it is not surprising that the largest single contributor to political campaigns during this period was in the health sector in Minnesota. From 1996 to 2004, the health industry contributed 29 percent of all industry-related funding to the legislative leadership in Minnesota (Broat et al. 2004). Although this amount is smaller than the proportion of licensing-related bills proposed in the legislature, it does reflect that industries that are most impacted by occupational licensing are more likely to contribute to influential individuals in the legislature. Funding for legislative leaders followed the occupational groups with the most at stake in the regulatory process. This approach is consistent with a capture theory view of occupational licensure, and the occupational associations perceive state regulation as an important arena for their members, and they attempt to directly impact legislation.

LICENSING AND QUALITY OF SERVICES IN MINNESOTA AND WISCONSIN

One of the major questions in the regulation of occupation literature is the institution's ability to increase the quality of service provided. The evolution of occupational licensing in Minnesota and Wisconsin allows for an examination of the quality effects of licensing versus certification, a less rigorous form of regulation. Wisconsin, which has tougher occupational regulations than Minnesota, is next to Minnesota geographically, has a similar population, income level, and unemployment rate. These similarities allow for a relevant comparison to examine the impact of different forms of regulation on one measure of service quality and on complaint rates to the regulatory body. If occupational licensing is successful relative to certification in accomplishing its objective of eliminating incompetent practitioners, lower-quality services are eliminated from the market and consumers are less likely to file complaints with state agencies.

The examination of these two similar states is instructive, especially since their policies on occupational licensing are different. The stated policy in Wisconsin is that it "favors regulation only when there is a

clear and direct harm to the public." Wisconsin has no "sunrise provision," which is legislation that requires that the burden of proof for
regulation is with the proponent of the regulation. On the other hand,
Minnesota has legislation labeled Chapter 214, which became termed
"sunrise legislation" and includes criteria for occupational regulation
against which any new or increased occupational regulation must be
judged and explicit questions that legislators and proponents of licensing must address (Office of the Legislative Auditor, State of Minnesota
1999). The regulatory policy articulated by Chapter 214 recognizes the
"potential danger of occupational restrictions and challenges proponents
of regulation to demonstrate that regulation serves the public interest"
(Office of the Legislative Auditor, State of Minnesota 1999). "Sunset
legislation," which eliminates regulation or reduces it, has not resulted
in the widespread success that it once seemed to promise and has never
been a regular part of the political process in Minnesota, which is generally perceived as a tougher state on occupational organizations seeking
regulation.

Using Department of Labor and Census definitions of licensing, it
is therefore not surprising that Wisconsin ranks sixth in the country in
the number of regulated occupations. It licenses 117 census-listed occupations covering 24 percent of its workforce, but Minnesota ranks
twenty-first and licenses 94 occupations covering only 13 percent of its
workforce in 2000. The ability to compare the impact of licensing versus certification is based on a comparison of physical therapists, respiratory care providers, and physician assistants (Broat et al. 2004). These
three health occupations are licensed in Wisconsin but were certified in
Minnesota[5] (Minnesota Board of Medical Practice 1993–2002; Wisconsin Department of Regulation and Licensing 2004). If an occupation is
certified, data are collected by the state on complaints about individuals
in the occupation, and all licensing boards must maintain data on complaints filed with the state licensing board.[6]

Figure 2.1 gives estimates of the complaint rate for Wisconsin relative to Minnesota. Either Minnesota has a more visible certification
board or there is a more litigious population in Minnesota relative to
Wisconsin. Evidence for a more litigious environment is that in 2003
Minnesota had a lawyer-to-population ratio of 1 attorney per 255 persons and Wisconsin had a ratio of 1 attorney per 396 persons, which is
a 63 percent lower rate of attorney coverage in Wisconsin (American

Figure 2.1 Regulatory Complaints in Wisconsin Compared to Minnesota

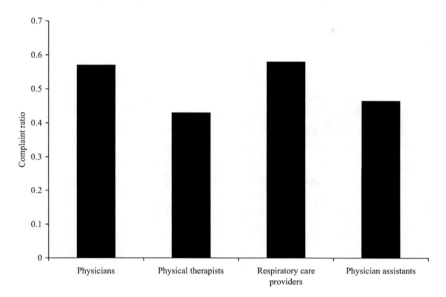

NOTE: These values are the summation of the rate of complaints to licensing boards in
Wisconsin divided by the number of complaints to certification boards in Minnesota
for physical therapists, respiratory care providers, and physician's assistants during
1999–2002. Physicians are licensed in both states.

SOURCE: Data from Broat et al. (2004) and Wisconsin Department of Regulation and
Licensing, 2004 and 2005.

Bar Association 2003; U.S. Census Bureau 2003). This larger ratio in
Minnesota could lead to a greater awareness of certain legal rights to
file complaints with regulatory boards. Moreover, filing a complaint
with an occupational certification board could be the first step in filing
a negligence suit against a member of the occupation. In all the occupations for which data in these two states are available, where one
of the occupations is certified and the other is licensed, Wisconsin had
a lower complaint value. Even for physicians, which is the longest licensed occupation in both states, Minnesota has a complaint rate that
is about twice as high as Wisconsin, even though Wisconsin's population is larger. There does not seem to be a meaningful difference in the
complaint rate of the certified occupations relative to the base rate of
the complaint rate for physicians in Minnesota, which is a state that

certified its occupations relative to Wisconsin that gave the same occupations a license to practice.

Figure 2.2 shows changes in the number of complaints to state
boards for these three occupations, which were certified in Minnesota
but licensed in Wisconsin, relative to physicians, who were licensed
in both states. In Wisconsin, physical therapists became fully licensed
with their own board in 1993, physician assistants moved from being
certified to licensed in 1997, and respiratory care providers became licensed in 1992 (Wisconsin Act 107 1993; Wisconsin Act 67 1997). The
initial low levels of complaints in the early period of licensing in Wisconsin are consistent with the hypothesis that initially tougher regulation increases quality as measured by this complaint data, but that over
time these quality impacts diminish or level off, and the level of complaints are similar to the certified occupations in Minnesota by the end
of the time period. The data plots show that the complaint rate declined
for physicians, the universally licensed occupation in both states, from
1994 to 2001. In contrast, for the three licensed occupations, physical

**Figure 2.2 Changes in Complaints in Certified and Licensed Occupations
in Minnesota and Wisconsin, 1994–2001**

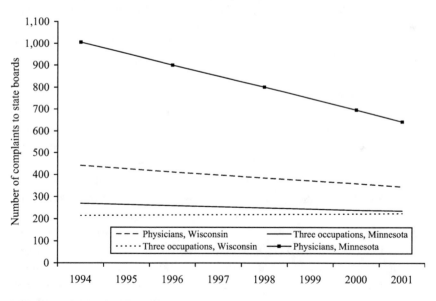

SOURCE: Data from Broat et al. (2004).

therapists, respiratory care providers, and physician assistants, in Wisconsin the complaint rate increased slightly over the same period. In Minnesota, where respiratory care providers and physician's assistants were certified over the entire period and for physical therapists who were certified until 1999, there was a small decline in the aggregate complaint rate during the same period. At a minimum, licensed occupations showed no greater ability to reduce constituents' complaints to licensing boards about the service provided compared to complaints filed in a regime where these same occupations were certified for most of the period. From the data provided in Figures 2.1 and 2.2 for these health-related occupations, there does not appear to be significant benefits for consumers of licensing relative to certification.

SUMMARY AND CONCLUSIONS

The goal of this chapter has been to present the development of occupational licensing as a labor market institution and show how this institution works within a state. Although the issue of occupational regulation often operates under the public policy radar screen, it has a long history in many different societies over time. There have been long periods where this institution has been pervasive and other times when there has been little to no occupational regulation by the government. One of the major issues for regulators and the public is whether the public interest theory of regulation has greater weight relative to the capture theory. If the public interest theory is dominant, occupational regulation reduces the likelihood that incompetent practitioners will enter an occupation and the public is protected from potential abuse. One outcome is that quality rises. But, if an occupation uses the regulatory process to limit competition and maintain or enhance the relative earnings of practitioners, with little impact on the quality received by consumers, then this labor market institution should be limited.

During different time periods, the impact of licensing may have resulted in both outcomes. Evidence suggests that licensing has positive impacts immediately following its implementation through the standardization of the quality of the service that is expected of practitioners. During this period, the ability to capture any economic monopoly rents may be limited as the occupation focuses on quality and providing voice to practitioners during the regulatory process. However, the returns to this process diminish over time, and the occupation focuses its efforts on restriction of supply through entry tests and other legal barriers that can limit the number of practitioners who enter the occupation from other regions. The apparent benefits of occupational regulation—providing higher quality as measured by a reduction in complaints—are not obvious, at least in the long run.

As an illustration of this process, this chapter examines Minnesota, a state that is in the middle of U.S. states in terms of its level of occupational regulation, using both the number of regulated occupations and the percentage of the workforce that is licensed. This state has experienced moderate growth in the number of occupations that are licensed, but the percentage of the state workforce that is covered by regulation has continued to grow, in large part as a consequence of the regulated occupations being in the fastest growing sector of the economy. In this state, occupations that spend the most on political campaigns are also the most regulated, evidence that is consistent with the political capture theory. The evidence from Minnesota's neighboring state of Wisconsin shows that licensing in that state versus certification in Minnesota provides no obvious benefits to consumers as measured by complaints to regulatory boards. The apparent benefits of occupational licensing relative to certification are not obvious, at least in the long run.

Studying data from just one state provides an in-depth look at regulation that includes the details of the licensing process. For example, focusing on a single state allows for a deeper understanding of new occupations seeking licensing. It also allows for a detailed examination of the allocation of meeting time for licensing boards. Further proposals to the state legislature for changing licensing provisions can be examined by observing how occupational lobbyists allocate funds for political purposes. The quality of services for licensed and unlicensed occupations can be examined in detail through state level analysis of nearby states. This depth of analysis does not give us enough breadth to examine the questions of quality versus restricting competition raised in this book. We now turn to a broader examination of the quality impacts of occupational licensing, followed by an examination of the potential restrictions of competition across states. The overarching questions of the policy implications of licensing are examined in detail in the chapters that follow.

Notes

1. For a more detailed history of licensing in the United States and in Europe, see *Occupational Licensing Legislation in the States* (Council of State Governments 1952).
2. There was a decline in the number of licensed occupational boards from the mid-1990s to 2004, a consequence of the consolidation of boards with few members following a report by the State Legislative Auditor recommending that occupations with few members be merged with larger boards.
3. The higher percentage of licensed workers in Minnesota reflects data gathered from state records from the regulatory agencies, which includes many occupations that are not listed by the Census Bureau in their listing of three-digit occupational titles. Consequently, estimates from the Department of Labor and the Census Bureau reflect a substantially downward-biased value relative to having state data from each regulatory agency. Nevertheless, the estimates presented in this paper reflect a consistent estimate since they use the same data-gathering approach for occupations and the same national database of the decennial censuses.
4. Leadership is defined as The Speaker of the House, House Majority Leader, House Majority Whip, House Assistant Majority Leader, House Minority Leader, House Minority Whip, House Assistant Minority Leader, Senate Majority Leader, Senate Assistant Majority Leader, Senate Majority Whip, Senate Minority Leader, and Senate Assistant Minority Leader. Political party leadership was acquired from the Minnesota House of Representatives (2004) and Senate Web sites. Committee membership was gathered from three bienniums using *The Minnesota Legislative Manual* (Minnesota Secretary of State 1997, 1999, 2001; Broat et al. 2004).
5. Physical therapists moved from certification to licensure in Minnesota during the period of analysis. The inclusion of this profession in the analysis is explained later in the methodology section.
6. The data collected for the number of complaints in Wisconsin come from D. O'Connell of the Wisconsin Department of Licensure and Regulation (personal communications, November 4, 2004, to Clint Pecenka). Conversely, data for the number of complaints in Minnesota were taken from the biennial reports of the regulation authority, in the case of the analyzed occupations, biennial reports of the Minnesota Board of Medical Practice (1993–2002). In all three occupations, the data available dictated the analysis of the years 1993–2002. During this time period, the data measure the number of complaints reported in each year (Broat et al. 2004).

3
Quality and the Demand for Occupational Licensing

Don't try this at home! Man does own root canals.

David Kruithoff is no dentist. He's a hired hand on a fruit farm outside of Lakeview, about an hour northeast of Grand Rapids. But that didn't stop him from performing two root canals on himself, then fashioning an entire set of replacement teeth.

—Tom Rademacher, *Ann Arbor News*, February 9, 1997

Although licensing is intended to increase quality of services and reduce the availability of substitutes, the newspaper story above illustrates an unintended consequence of the licensing of dental services, namely using do-it-yourself remedies. The individual highlighted in this newspaper column had no dental health insurance and stated that the cost of going to a dentist was just too much for his limited budget. Most of the research on the regulation of occupations has emphasized barriers to entry, but relatively little empirical work has examined the quality of output or the demand-side response by consumers to these quality effects. This chapter focuses on why and how service outcomes are affected by licensing statutes or other administrative procedures. It also examines how regulation of some occupations results in better outcomes for individuals with better insurance coverage but has little impact for individuals who have few other work-related benefits. Another aspect examined is the interaction of the changes in technology and capital requirements within the regulated service on standardization and the quality of service delivery to consumers. This is an advantage of regulation that many professional associations argue guarantees a higher average level of service with licensing.

Initially, this chapter presents theoretical rationales for why individuals seek to license their occupations, and why policymakers are likely to grant this form of regulation for the members of the trade. The next section shows how licensing can have both benefits and costs for the consumers of the regulated service, and it presents new evidence regarding who gains from regulation. The following portion of the chapter gives a review of previous studies of the quality and price impacts of licensing on consumers. This section focuses on how licensing may serve as a method of screening potential practitioners that can have beneficial outcomes.

WHY ARE OCCUPATIONS REGULATED?

Licensing is assumed to affect demand through controls on entry, and this impacts quality (Benham 1980). The expectation from economic theory is that licensing may create windfall gains or rents, and that these prospective gains in income provide an important impetus for licensure. The threat of loss of rents is a major reason why removal of licensure is so strongly resisted by members of a regulated occupation. Another benefit to practitioners is the ability of licensing to provide some hedge against downside risks because of the organization's ability to reduce competition differentially when conditions are bad (Wheelan 1999). Licensed occupations are able to limit supply in response to market conditions through changing licensing statutes or through extending the required training program for entry or reducing the numbers who pass an entrance exam. Moreover, Ballou and Podgursky (1998) argue in the case of teachers that lengthening the period of time that it takes to become a teacher results in otherwise qualified applicants seeking other unregulated occupations that have fewer legal restrictions. The end result is that lower-qualified individuals with fewer labor market opportunities become teachers.

A major theoretical justification for licensing is that there are market failures due to asymmetric information on quality between producers and consumers that regulation can correct. Such failures can occur if it is more difficult for consumers than sellers to determine the quality of a service offered. Generally, licensed occupations claim that they will successfully cope with such undesirable market failures. Many of the occupations provide training programs to their new and continuing members that highlight the important benefits to the public of licensing their occupation (Benham 1980).

The structure of the market may also result in the demand for licensing being lower than optimum because of potential "free rider" problems that occur because consumers purchase professional services infrequently (Cox and Foster 1990). Consequently, an individual consumer may incur high costs learning about a particular profession and determining which type of regulation is in their best interests. Moreover, the costs of taking action may be high, since there are large costs associated with informing and organizing a large group of consumers to take action. Many may not join groups to obtain the optimum amount of occupational regulation because they think that others may take group action. This is the case if the purchase price of the service was low. As a result consumers would rarely demand either occupational licensure or higher forms of regulation or lobby against restrictions.

In contrast, the "capture theory" suggests that the individuals in the occupations often expend considerable resources in an attempt to convince legislators that regulation will benefit the public. The capture theory of occupational regulation argues that licensing is a response by professionals who seek to protect themselves from competition. If demand for the service is relatively inelastic, then higher prices will lead to higher incomes. Moreover, occupational regulation also could be viewed as a form of career insurance. If regulation reduces competition, members of the regulated occupation are less likely to be forced out and trained for another occupation. The prediction from microeconomics is that the less the elasticity of demand for the occupation's services, the greater the benefit of regulation to the members of the occupation (Stigler 1971). Consequently, the theory would predict that the benefits of regulation to dentists, for example, would be greater than that for barbers or cosmetologists because the availability of substitutes for dental care, even including those who give themselves root canals, would be lower than for cutting hair.

The demand for regulation by the individuals in licensed professions is less likely to be affected by the kind of "free-rider" problem faced by consumers. Individuals in the occupations have a greater interest in and knowledge of regulation affecting their line of work than most consumers of licensed services, and the occupational associations have a greater ability to act together. Consequently, the costs of organizing behind a type of regulation for members of an occupation are relatively less than for consumers, and the benefits to individuals in the occupation are likely to be higher. Even though there are incentives for both consumers and producers of the service to demand regulation, consumers are rarely the moving force behind occupational regulation, possibly because of the issues cited above. Members of the occupations generally demand licensing laws at least in part due to the potential benefits of higher pay and job security.

Although these theories give reasons for why persons in occupations may want to become regulated, they do not give the rationale for the demand for licensing by states or other political entities, such as cities or counties (Wheelan 1999). Competing theories for the existence of licensing from the public perspective generally involve conflicts between "public interest" and "rent-capture" rationales for regulation. If the public interest is the dominant rationale for licensing, occupations with the greatest risk to the public—either to the person employing the service or to a third party—should be the most likely to be regulated. On the other hand, a political rationale of the demand for licensing requires that the professional association be well-organized and well-funded to carry out a licensing campaign at the appropriate political level. Although most licensing is at the state level, construction-related regulations impacting plumbers, painters, and carpenters often occur with divergent standards at the city or county level (Shimberg, Esser, and Kruger 1973). Moreover, such a campaign is likely to be more successful if the consumers are individuals rather than larger institutions such as hospitals (Graddy 1991). In his analysis of which occupations are licensed in the state of Illinois, Wheelan finds support for both the public interest and rent-capture theories discussed above. Occupations with higher insurance premiums, which indicate greater risk to the public, are more likely to be regulated, indicating support for the public interest model. However, an organization's number of members and budget, as well as client type (personal versus institutional), all show support for the rent-capture rationale for licensing the profession. For example, for physicians, Paul (1984) states that "licensing legislation was the result of organized physicians employing the political system for limiting entry and the concomitant increasing of returns to incumbent medical practitioners." A further illustration of this process is the growth in secondary housing mortgage markets, and the more than sixfold increase of mortgage brokers from 8,500 in 1988 to more than 53,000 in 2004. The state occupational regulation of mortgage loan officers grew from a few in the late 1980s to 24 in 2004 (Reed 2005; Wholesale Access Mortgage Research and Consulting Inc. 2005).

An alternative explanation for the rationale for benefits and costs of attempting to enter an occupation comes from the "club model," which purports to show the rationale for nonprofit organizations engaging in exclusive behavior and having especially high time costs of entry (Iannaccone 1992). Occupations can limit entry as a method to "signal" quality and to show both those in the occupation and outsiders that individuals are committed to the work of the occupation (Spence 1973). "Signaling" explains apparent inefficiency—time and money "wasted" to acquire a college degree or "irrational" attachments to honesty, loyalty, or the giving of "inefficient presents" such as certificates or licenses rather than cash (Frank 1988). This in part explains the high entry costs and initiation rights that are often required of licensed occupations as well as the exclusive nature of this form of regulation, where individuals not in the "club" are precluded from working in the field. Further, these time costs can screen out people whose participation in the occupation otherwise would be marginal, while at the same time increasing participation among those who remain, thereby increasing the perceived quality of the individuals in the occupation. Individuals who want to enter an occupation must exhibit the resiliency of the potential shame costs of the stigma of failing an exam and the self-sacrifice of schooling, time spent studying for and taking licensing exams, residency requirements, and oaths of loyalty and honesty (Kandel and Lazear 1992).

A further explanation of the societal benefits and costs of licensing can be found in the theory presented by Hirschman (1970) and then applied by Freeman and Medoff (1984) to explain how unions can have both a positive "voice effect" on productivity and a negative "monopoly effect." A similar approach also could be applied to occupational regulation. The monopoly face of licensing is generally presented as the principal outcome of regulation by most economists (Rottenberg 1980). However, to the extent that licensing requires (through continuing education) that its members discuss and promote positive aspects of their work experience, disseminate information about how to do the job better, require job-specific training, promote ethical standards, or devise methods of adjudicating disputes between consumers and producers, all of these policies have the ability to promote "high performance workplace practices" within the occupation. On the other hand, using the government to restrict supply in order to increase prices for the services offered, which in turn increases wages, would be the central element of the "monopoly face" of occupational licensing. A third element deals with the extent to which regulation impacts exiting from the occupation if the economic or social standing of the work substantially declined. Perhaps the "club model" discussed above requires sufficiently large time commitments upon entry, and this may result in relatively few persons leaving these licensed occupations over time. Unlike unionization, where employees can lose their jobs in the unionized setting and find other ones in the nonunion sector, licensed workers may be more likely to maintain their regulated status throughout their working lives.

This variety of explanations for why occupations seek to become regulated provides many reasons for having this labor market institution. Each suggests why occupational licensing may either ensure quality for consumers or provide practitioners with greater monopoly rents and higher labor market status. Whether any of these explanations of the benefits or costs of regulation dominate needs to be examined with data and analysis.

HOW LICENSING AFFECTS QUALITY

If there are incentives for occupations to restrict supply and create barriers to entry, then what are the consequences for consumers of the regulated service? Figure 3.1 shows the anticipated process of how occupational regulation may impact service quality. Starting with the box to the left labeled "Regulation," the figure shows how regulation operates through state-level pass rates, more restrictive licensing statutes, and reciprocity agreements with other states to restrict the entry of new practitioners. For example, licensing boards react to changes in consumer demand by changing administrative procedures through the pass rate for new entrants or by establishing residency requirements for persons coming from other states (Kleiner 1990; Maurizi 1974). The figure shows that the consequences of restricting entry to an occupation in any period occurring in the second box, labeled "Flow of licensed practitioners," are to reduce supply and increase the prices of the regulated service, as shown by the plus sign beside the box marked "Prices."

Figure 3.1 Regulation's Impact on Net Quality

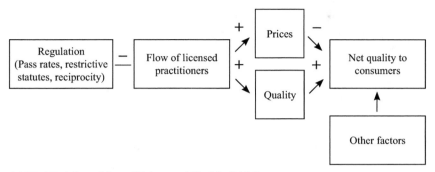

SOURCE: Adapted from Kleiner and Kudrle (2000).

Similar regulatory factors that are shown in the figure are presumed to influence the quality of the service. Assuming that lower-quality practitioners are prohibited from entry because restrictions are increased, as shown on the bottom portion of Figure 3.1 labeled "Quality," the mean quality of the service received is increased, since the remaining practitioners entering the occupation are of higher quality as measured by test scores and evidence of "greater moral character." A further illustration of the impact of increasing entry restrictions on the quality of practitioners is shown in Figure 3.2. As the pass rate is reduced or the educational requirements are increased, the mean quality of practitioners in the occupation is increased. An increase in requirements increases the minimum competence from level A to B. As a consequence of licensing, the average quality of practitioners shifts to the right from point C, the average quality when restrictions are at A, to D when restrictions are at level B along this bell-shaped curve in the figure. With this presumed enhancement in quality, the use of services would increase as perceived quality of the service grew among consumers. In the absence of any theory or evidence to the contrary, I assume that the stringency of professionally administered quality controls such as licensure is the best proxy for quality as recognized by the consumer of the service. This factor alone would increase service quality as shown in Figure 3.1, as increases in net quality to consumers (through the plus sign of flows) and lead to overall enhancement of net quality to consumers. On the other hand, higher service prices would reduce the overall ser-

Figure 3.2 Impact of Increasing Standards on Competence and Quality

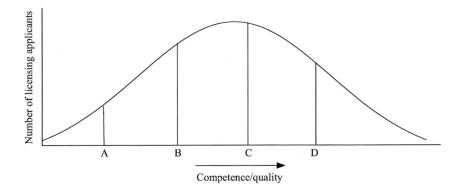

SOURCE: Adapted from Holen (1978).

vice rendered, as fewer consumers would use the service as price rises. Consequently, those who receive the service would benefit through higher-quality services, but lower-income individuals might not receive the service because prices would rise under licensing. The net effect of regulation on service quality is therefore theoretically unclear.

Professor Carl Shapiro presents a theoretical model in which he argues that licensing benefits those who can afford higher-quality services, typically individuals with higher incomes or those with insurance coverage for the service, and consequently the real service price is low (Shapiro 1986). Table 3.1 presents econometric evidence of a statistical application of this theory for dental services. The estimates show results that are consistent with the general theoretical model of who gains from tougher licensing. The data use medical and demographic information from a sample of 464 new enlistees into the U.S. Air Force (Kleiner and Kudrle 2000). The data contained complete information from their initial exams in the U.S. Air Force, along with self-reported demographic and economic information, as well as their dental histories. The demographic and economic values of individuals in this sample are consistent with those of individuals of a similar age from the Current Population Survey (CPS) from the 1990s. The dependent variable in this analysis is the dollar value of untreated deterioration divided by the total depreciation of the individuals' dental condition. The table is divided into two columns. The first shows regression estimates where the dependent

Table 3.1   Estimates of the Impact of Tougher Licensing Regulations and Dental Insurance Coverage on the Dollar Value of Untreated Dental Deterioration[a]

	With insurance coverage ($N = 269$)[b]	Without insurance coverage ($N = 195$)[b]
High regulation	−0.14[c]	−0.03
	(0.06)	(0.09)

[a] Sample includes 464 new recruits into the U.S. Air Force.
[b] Estimates include controls for income, education, and gender. Standard errors, in parentheses, include corrections for group bias.
[c] Indicates statistical significance at the 95% confidence interval.

variable results are truncated. These use Tobit estimates of the impact of tougher licensing requirements for dentists for individuals who have insurance coverage. The estimates in the table include demographic controls for individual and household characteristics. The second column gives estimates for persons who did not have coverage with the same statistical control variables. The results in column one show that individuals in states with relatively high regulation for dentists and insurance coverage have lower untreated dental deterioration. In column two the estimates show that higher regulation has no statistically significant impact on service outcomes when there is no insurance coverage. Perhaps for individuals whose price of dental services is high, they choose to use lesser amounts of these services. Further, these estimates are consistent with earlier results showing that individuals with higher education and larger incomes have lower untreated dental deterioration in the same national sample of new U.S. Air Force recruits (Kleiner and Kudrle 2000). These results show that individuals with lower perceived prices through insurance or higher incomes are better off with tougher state regulations within dentistry.

Similarly, a study by Maurizi (1980) shows that higher standards of regulation of construction contractors serve to enhance quality for large, relatively well-off consumers. Although the net impacts of occupational licensing may be negative for all users of the service, for certain segments of the population, namely those individuals with higher incomes or insurance coverage, this form of regulation results in higher quality. Moreover, licensing may further serve to exacerbate the variation in the relative quality of service received or "consumption" by lower-income individuals relative to those with higher incomes or for individuals covered by insurance (Attanasio et al. 2002).

RESULTS OF STUDIES ON THE BENEFITS OF OCCUPATIONAL REGULATION

The basic relationships shown in Figure 3.1 would suggest that the quality of a service would be negatively related to the pass rate in a state, but that these regulations may also raise the skill of the service provider, since that person must spend additional time learning occupation-related skills. Studies of demand have attempted to overcome the problem of variability in outcomes by making quality adjustments based on occupation human capital characteristics of the persons providing the service. However, there is no assurance that the services actually received by consumers are positively correlated with these proxy measures of input productivity, and the distinction between the number of inputs employed and the quality of outputs received may not be consistent. For example, a less-competent dentist may require multiple attempts to fill a tooth to the same standard that a more-skilled dentist could accomplish at once. Furthermore, there is little to no published research on the relationship between performance on the licensing exam and an individual's ability to perform on the job.[1] Even for occupations with lower general education requirements (e.g., cosmetology), job-specific training is usually longer than one year, with an apprenticeship followed by a state-licensing exam.

Nevertheless, several research studies have attempted to develop methods of estimating the impact of licensing on quality or the demand for licensed services. Table 3.2 shows information from many major academic studies of the impact of licensing on quality and on consumers.[2] For the benefits of licensing there are a disproportionate number of studies on regulation in dentistry and education. This is partly because, for many years, dentistry had large variations in state licensing requirements and unique state-specific requirements, such as the "gold foil" method of filling teeth that was required in California. Moreover, outcome measures like cavities were easy to identify and quantify. Dollar values across political jurisdictions were generally available. Two of

Table 3.2 Studies on Benefits of Licensing in the United States: Quality and Demand Effects

Authors	Occupation	Finding
Holen (1978)	Dentists	Licensing reduces the likelihood of adverse outcomes and increases the quality of care.
Maurizi (1980)	Contractors	Circumvention of minimum competency requirements, which allows lower-than-minimum-quality contractors to obtain licenses, may reduce the potential quality effects of licensing.
Carroll and Gaston (1981)	Electricians, dentists, plumbers, real estate agents, optometrists, sanitarians, and veterinarians	Licensing increases the quality of individual practitioners but lowers the overall quality of services received by decreasing the total stock of practitioners.
Shapiro (1986)	Licensed occupations	Licensing benefits the segment of consumers that values quality highly.
Kleiner and Petree (1988)	Teachers	Licensing has uncertain effects on student achievement scores.
Kleiner and Kudrle (2000)	Dentists	Tougher licensing has no effect on the overall quality of outputs, but higher income groups benefit from tougher standards.
Angrist and Guryan (2003)	Teachers	State-mandated teacher testing has no effect on teacher quality.
Kane, Rockoff, and Staiger (2005)	Teachers	Little difference in student achievement between students taught by licensed, unlicensed, or alternative certified teachers in the same schools in New York City.
Kane and Staiger (2005)	Teachers	No evidence that licensed teachers are more effective than those without traditional credentials in raising student achievement in Los Angeles.

the cited studies in Table 3.2 show conflicting outcomes of the impact of licensing on the quality of care. For example, Holen (1978) finds that licensing reduces the likelihood of adverse outcomes and increases the quality of care, but Carroll and Gaston (1981) find it diminishes quality, and Kleiner and Kudrle (2000) find no effect. Since Holen and Carroll and Gaston use the same data source gathered from the naval recruits, the differences in the outcomes rely largely on different measures of outcomes. Holen uses a measure of the condition of the teeth itself, such as cavities or if there are broken or chipped teeth. On the other hand, Carroll and Gaston use a measure of an oral hygiene index, which focuses on the soft tissue and includes measures such as gum disease. The Kleiner and Kudrle study uses measures of dental health, which incorporate Holen's measure as well as the ones by Carroll and Gaston, and also uses a "quality-adjusted" pass rate as well as statutory factors. Kleiner and Kudrle's analysis also uses a broader number of controls for economic and demographic factors. Using these updated and more refined measures of dental condition, the characteristics of the individuals in the study, and measures of regulation by the states, they find no impact of tougher state licensing laws and administrative procedures on measures of dental condition.

Studies of other occupations listed in Table 3.2 range from construction contractors to teachers and suggest that tougher forms of regulation have murky effects on quality or the demand for the service (Angrist and Guryan 2003; Kane, Rockoff, and Staiger 2005; Kleiner and Petree 1988; Maurizi 1980; Shapiro 1986). For contractors, Maurizi finds that allowing lower-quality contractors to obtain licenses would reduce the quality-enhancing impacts of this type of labor market regulation. In education, the growth of occupational licensing requirements over the past two decades has resulted in uncertain effects on student test scores in New York City and Los Angeles (Kane, Rockoff, and Staiger 2005; Kane and Staiger 2005), a generally recognized measure of "quality" in education. Carrolll and Gaston (1981) study seven widely varying licensed occupations and find that licensing has either a negative or no impact on the quality of services received by consumers. However, using a theoretical model of the impacts of licensing, Shapiro argues that licensing should be thought of by income segments of the consumer market for licensed services. The argument is that wealthier consumers who value quality more highly gain the benefits, but lower-income individuals with lesser relative demand for quality services would lose from tougher licensing standards by having less access to the service (Shapiro 1986).

Another factor in the growth of the demand for licensing is its disproportionate prevalence in medical service delivery. Consumption of medical services grew by 25 percent as a percentage of all consumer purchases from 1984 to 1995 (Ford and Ginsburg 2001). Moreover, the prices of medical services have risen more rapidly than overall prices in the economy (Triplett 2001). An important factor in the growth of this sector has been that technological change has grown much more rapidly in the medical industry than it has for other services in the economy, leading to a need for more standardized labor inputs (Fixler and Ginsburg 2001). Licensing has fulfilled this demand for a minimum requirement of standardization as a complementary input to the rapid technological change in this industry.

In one of the few field studies of the impacts of licensing on quality, the FTC examined the relationship between licensing and the overprescription of services (Phelan 1974). In this study, televisions with known defects were used to determine the incidents of oversubscribed services in three locations: Washington, D.C., which has no licensing of television repair; New Orleans, Louisiana, which licenses individuals; and San Francisco, California, which licenses the facility but not the individual. One of the findings was that "the Louisiana Licensing Law does not protect the consumer from what has been defined as 'parts fraud'" (Phelan 1974). The estimates from the study found that parts fraud was about 20 percent in San Francisco, compared to about 50 percent in New Orleans and Washington, D.C. Therefore, licensing of individuals may not be an optimal method of consumer protection relative to no licensing or the regulation of a business.

In another field study on optical care conducted by the FTC, Kwoka (1984) finds that the average quality of eye care is lower in regions with restrictions on advertising. Moreover, Liang and Ogur (1987) find that licensing rules that restrict the use of dental hygienists and assistants increased the average price of a dental visit by 11 percent in 1970 and 7 percent in 1982. They suggest that, if these price increases do not produce any quality benefits, then consumers are worse off. There could be benefits of such regulations if having higher-quality dentists perform screening exams on patients enables the discovery of dental disease or problems that left untreated could result in long-term problems of teeth and gum deterioration. Generally, the licensing literature attributes the total increase in the price of the service to inefficiencies of regulation and economic rents. However, part of this increase could reflect an increase in quality or a shift outward in the demand curve for the service with a resulting increase in price.

Overall, few of these studies of demand and quality show significant benefits of occupational regulation. However, a most convincing study would provide a randomized experiment of consumers going to unregulated versus regulated service providers and then measure the outcomes of the service. Unfortunately, this type of analysis has not been implemented. Instead most analyses of licensing reviewed in this chapter analyze more highly regulated regimes relative to less-regulated ones. In these cases the results show that licensing has modest to no effects on the demand for the service or on the quality of service received by consumers. From this evidence there is little to show that occupational regulation has a major effect on the quality of service received by consumers or on the demand for the service other than thorough potential price effects.

QUALITY EFFECTS AS MEASURED THROUGH INSURANCE PREMIUMS

One method of determining whether licensing has an impact on the quality of a service is through the premiums charged to individuals in regulated and unregulated states. The rationale for this evaluation is that if licensing serves to keep out incompetent potential practitioners relative to states that do not have licensing, then there would be a reduction in lawsuits, which in turn could lead to lower premiums. In discussions with officials at the Chubb Insurance Company, their view was that licensing makes an occupation more visible and sets up rules and regulations that make lawsuits easier to file. The impact of this more structured procedure would drive up premiums. The greater visibility of the occupation and the greater ability to file lawsuits due to licensing's structure compensate for any benefits from the quality aspects of licensing from the perspective of the insurance industry.

In order to analyze whether licensing reduces malpractice insurance rates, I examined three occupations that are regulated in some states and not in others. In the first case I examined occupational therapists, which are licensed in approximately half of all states. I then filed online for malpractice insurance for an occupational therapist, age 35, with greater than three years of experience for the highest level of coverage. The exercise showed there was no difference in the rates in the states that licensed occupational therapists versus those states where the occupation was certified or unregulated. Secondly, I then looked at practical and vocational nurses, which require licensing in 46 states. I then checked the malpractice insurance rates for a 35-year-old full-time nurse through the Nurses Service Organization. The company is the nation's largest provider of professional liability insurance coverage for nurses, with over 650,000 nursing professionals insured nationally. The premiums in the four states (Arizona, Arkansas, Maryland, and Washington) that did not license practical and licensed vocational nurses were no higher than the ones that licensed them. The last group examined was clinical psychologists, who are generally licensed. Using the same methodology, there was no difference in the malpractice rates across states. However, the insurance company had an explicit policy that they would only insure psychologists with a master's degree and a license or someone who had a PhD in psychology. This was the only case where there was evidence that the insurance industry valued a licensed professional relative to an unlicensed one in the data that was examined for this analysis.

In order to further examine the impact of licensing on malpractice insurance, I present the results from additional statistical evidence on occupations that are regulated in some states and not in others. Using data for pastoral counselors, marriage and family therapists, and professional counselors, Cordes (2005) examined whether insurance premiums are lower in states that license these three occupations. Professional counselors are the largest of the three occupations, with more than 52,000 members (American Counseling Association 2005). Marriage and family therapy has less than half that with an estimated 23,000 members (American Association for Marriage and Family Therapy 2005). By far the smallest of the three occupations analyzed is pastoral counseling, with just over 3,000 individuals linked to the primary association (American Association of Pastoral Counselors 2005). The data used in the analysis were taken from insurance premiums published in tables on the Internet by the American Professional Agency (2005). The organization is the largest writer of mental health liability insurance in the United States (American Professional Agency 2005). The level of regulation varies greatly across these three occupations. For example, only four states license pastoral counselors, but more than 40 states license both professional counselors and marriage and family counselors. By analyzing these three occupations both individually and in aggregate, the analysis attempts to statistically examine the impact of being in a state that licenses an occupation on malpractice insurance rates for 2005 (Cordes 2005). Cordes is careful to use the same level of malpractice coverage for each state as well as similar age and experience data to calculate state rates. Using this data, Cordes estimates regression equations and finds that "Ultimately, the estimates both for individual professions and in the comprehensive model do not show a significant relationship between the key variables of licensing or certification regulation and malpractice insurance premiums" (Cordes 2005, p. 23). Using insurance malpractice premiums as a measure of quality shows no impact of licensing on reducing the risk of a high payout as measured by the insurance industry for any of these three occupations or for the other occupations for which I could obtain insurance premium data.

One argument that licensing may enhance quality goes as follows: when an occupation becomes regulated, documented standardization may make it a target of lawsuits. The evidence that premiums do not go up may suggest that licensing does increase quality to compensate for the increased visibility of the occupation to attorneys. However, there are no data to support the hypothesis that lawsuits disproportionately target regulated occupations because of licensing. Consequently, from the available data and analysis there is no evidence that licensing enhances quality as measured by complaints to state boards or through lower malpractice insurance premiums. Nevertheless, perhaps with more information on insurance claims or greater detail on the types of complaints to state boards, a more complete answer on the quality effects of licensing could be estimated.

ESTIMATES OF THE PRICE IMPACTS

Most estimates of the impacts of licensing policies on price of the service show positive impacts (Cox and Foster 1990). Table 3.3 shows the effect of licensing practices on prices for various services. These practices range from restrictions on interstate mobility by limiting reciprocity to restrictions on advertising and other commercial practices (Bond et al. 1980; Feldman and Begun 1978; Shepard 1978). The impact of licensing-related practices on prices ranges from 4 to 35 percent, depending on the type of commercial practice and location. The rationale for these impacts on raising prices could be that government regulations reduce uncertainty or the likelihood of poor service or "lemons" in the market (Akerloff 1970). As a consequence, consumers perceive the service to be of higher quality and demand more of the service, driving up the price. On the other hand, regulations could be a form of rent capture by the incumbent practitioners by limiting entry or restricting price information in the market for the service (Friedman 1962b, p. 223). By government granting a monopoly in the market for the service, the long-term impact would be lower-quality service and higher prices. From the empirical studies of licensing, it is difficult to tell which of these effects dominates in the determination of the rise of prices for licensed services. However, a consequence for regulated occupations with high incomes, like dentists and lawyers, is the ability to raise prices through the impacts of regulation with few readily available substitutes. This monopoly power may reallocate income from lower-income customers to higher-income practitioners.

An alternative explanation of these price increases often given by the occupations' professional associations is that the method of delivering services for the profession has changed over time, allowing a group of experts to supervise, govern, and recommend changes that would standardize the practices. The result would be that average quality per practitioner would go up, and this would be reflected in higher-quality services as reflected in price rises. Further, capital expenditures have increased, requiring higher prices to capture a return on investment for either a sole practitioner or for an HMO (Cutler and Berndt 2001). On the other hand, standardization may also stifle innovation or new tech-

Table 3.3 Studies on Price Effects of Licensing

Authors	Occupation	Finding
Benham (1972)	Optometry	Advertising restrictions increase the price of eyeglasses by 25 percent.
Cady (1976)	Pharmacy	Price advertising restrictions increase prices by approximately 5 percent.
Feldman and Begun (1978, 1980)	Optometry	Prices are 9–16 percent higher in states that restrict advertising by opticians and/or optometrists, with larger effects in states that restrict advertising by both occupations.
Shepard (1978)	Dentistry	Reciprocity restrictions raise the price of dental services approximately 15 percent.
Bond et al. (1980)	Optometry	Average eye exam and eyeglass prescription is 35 percent more expensive in cities with restrictive commercial practices for optometrists.
Bond et al. (1980)	Legal	Restrictions on advertising result in a 5–11 percent increase in price, depending on the particular legal service rendered.
Conrad and Sheldon (1982)	Dentistry	Restrictions on the number of branch offices and the use of dental hygienists each result in a 4 percent increase in price.
Kwoka (1984)	Optometry	Restrictions on advertising and commercial practices, such as an optometrist working for an optical firm, increase price by 20 percent with no decline in quality.
Haas-Wilson (1986)	Optometry	Commercial practice restrictions, which restrict the employment of optometrists by nonprofessional corporation, the locations of optometrists' offices, the operation of branch offices, and the use of trade names by optometrists employed by nonprofessional corporations, result in a 5–13 percent increase in price with no commensurate increase in quality.
Liang and Ogur (1987)	Dentistry	Restrictions on the number of hygienists that a dentist may employ increase the average price of a dental visit 7 percent. The restriction cost consumers approximately $700 million in 1982.

Authors	Occupation	Finding
Kleiner and Kudrle (2000)	Dentists	Tougher licensing, as measured by the pass rate or the overall measure of restrictiveness of the state, is associated with an increase in prices. A state that changed from low or medium to highest restrictiveness could expect to see an 11 percent increase in the price of dental services.
Federal Trade Commission (2002)	Opticians	The average price of a six-lens multipack purchased via mail order is 19 percent less than the average price for lenses purchased from ophthalmologists, optometrists, and optical chains.

niques of practice by not allowing new procedures to be introduced because they fly in the face of standard procedures.

A further reason for the price increases is that the complexity of the science and practice in most of these occupations has skyrocketed over the past 50 years (Cutler and Berndt 2001). The complexity requires that only individuals with high levels of training and expertise can determine whether other individuals are competent to perform in the occupation. Beyond being a boon to industrial psychologists, who must develop and administer these government-required exams, members of the occupation are involved in the development of the exams and other requirements to determine the minimum required level of competence and continuing education requirements. To the extent that these individuals can identify this expertise, the quality of work in the occupation is higher, but consumers may have a higher standard and quality level than they would want, relative to a regime of certification.

To illustrate, college professors are certified through their educational attainment but not licensed. Consequently, universities can hire non-PhD teachers and researchers without financial or criminal penalties by the government. Further, members of the occupation have a voice in the determination of the minimum level of competence for continued employment. Although there are also opportunities for abuse, the argument for this type of system allows for oversight, but individuals without PhDs can be part of the system without government penalties. If quality is not maintained, the status of the educational institution falls, with a subsequent decline in the attendance of high-ability students and research funding.

SUMMARY AND CONCLUSIONS

This chapter has provided a background for analyzing the potential benefits of occupational licensing as a labor market institution and its effects on the demand for the regulated service. The theories of the demand for occupational regulation show quality-enhancing policies that improve the perception of the service in the eyes of the consumer and allow the public to eliminate individuals who are not competent to perform a service. Giving the members of the occupation a voice in the organization of service delivery is expected to enhance the productivity of the members of the regulated occupation. Further, establishing long training periods and rigorous entry standards provides evidence of a strong commitment to the profession. In addition, for those states where the occupation is well-organized and well-funded, they are more likely to obtain statutory regulations for the occupation. Theory suggests that regulation is able to increase the quality of practitioners by limiting the number of lower-quality practitioners through testing and statutory requirements. This outcome may be moderated by some persons with other opportunities choosing another occupation rather than spending the time seeking licensing. Consequently, the average quality in the occupation is generally higher, but there are fewer licensed practitioners to service consumer demand, which drives up prices or the wait time for the service. However, whether consumers gain from occupational licensing is a question that is still open to empirical analysis, but thus far, the preponderance of evidence suggests no impact.

Licensing appears to be complementary with growth in technology. As capital and technological growth has increased in occupations like medicine and dentistry, higher-quality labor and standardized labor inputs are required. One method of this standardization is the granting of monopoly power to the professions to ensure this higher average level of service quality reduces the number of poor performers. Through continuing education requirements, additional certification for specialization, and testing for basic skills, licensing provides a standardized labor input that may be complementary with increasing technology and innovation.

The analysis of studies of licensed occupations finds that the impact of regulation on the quality of service received by consumers is murky, with most of the studies of this issue showing no effects on average consumer well-being relative to little or no regulation. On the other hand, most of the studies of licensing find that prices are higher for services with higher levels of regulation. From these studies of occupational regulation, it appears that higher-price effects dominate potential modest impacts on quality. Consequently, occupational licensing's effect is generally negative on consumer well-being. However, for higher-income consumers regulation may result in higher-quality services. An additional reason for the increase in prices is that there have been technological changes within many of the regulated occupations and that these prices reflect the increased training, greater technology, and innovations that have occurred in the occupations.

However, one important counterfactual has not been analyzed: the impact of no regulation on contributing to a major catastrophic outcome such as the spread of disease or the collapse of a building because of incompetent workers or inspectors. Consequently, the benefits of regulating who works may still be positive if it reduces the chances of a large loss to the public relative to other ways of guarding public health and safety. Although there are many anecdotes that document worker negligence or incompetence that have led to major serious injury or even deaths, there is little evidence that licensing would have eliminated serious tragedies in any systematic manner.[3]

Notes

1. Since licensure tests are not trying to measure performance but rather competence, there has been virtually no work on this topic by psychologists (Sackett 2004). The American Psychological Association (1999) notes that for licensure testing, one relies on "content validity" (does the test sample a specified "content domain") as opposed to "criterion-related validity" (does the test correlate with subsequent performance).
2. Given the diversity of occupations and methods used, meta analysis would be a difficult and perhaps even inappropriate way to obtain an overall value of the demand or quality effects of licensing.
3. Examples of worker incompetence include a Staten Island ferry crash during October 2003, and a New York City subway crash in June 1995, both of which involved licensed workers who failed to follow established standards for the operation of the machinery.

4
Licensing, Labor Supply, and Earnings

Advocates of teacher professionalization are unapologetic about the prospects of higher salaries. In their view, the nation has undervalued the services teachers provide and has not spent enough to recruit and retain good teachers. If high standards compel state and local governments to increase teacher salaries, that is only what they ought to have done anyway. In short, proponents of professional self-regulation argue that the reforms they advocate represent a "win-win" solution to some of the nation's educational ills: good for teachers and good for the rest of the country.

—Dale Ballou and Michael Podgursky in "Gaining Control of Professional Licensing and Advancement" (2000, p. 82)

As this analysis suggests, advocates of "teacher professionalization" seek to not only increase the quality of education, but also to raise the earnings of the members of the occupation through tougher regulations. The task of licensing is generally placed with state licensing boards, which usually consist of individuals in the occupation with an understandable incentive to restrict entry and drive up earnings. Moreover, choosing only the most able to practice also may serve to increase the average level of human capital within the occupation. This chapter discusses the why and how of occupational regulations' ability to restrict supply and the implications for the earnings of practitioners. Although our method of analysis cannot tell conclusively that any earnings effects are due solely to supply- or demand-driven factors, the analysis establishes certain facts regarding licensing and earnings for certain occupations. One of the methods of analysis uses the counterfactual of how much individuals in these occupations would earn if they did not have a license. Moreover, further analysis examines how changes in regulatory statutes and administrative procedures impact earnings.

A perspective on occupational licensing suggests that it is "diagnostic and inexpensive to administer, they impose minimal costs on those who are actually competent, but present a serious obstacle to those who are not" (Camerer et al. 2003). Although this may be the case with a driver's license as discussed in Chapter 1, it is not the case for licensed occupations. Entering an occupation such as dentistry or law requires at least seven years beyond high school, at least three of which are spent in occupation-specific training. Pass rates can vary by more than 25 percent by state, and exams often are given only twice a year. Failure to pass an exam may result in considerable shame and guilt costs on individuals, either discouraging them from entering the occupation or prompting them to choose another state in which to practice (Kandel and Lazear 1992). Unlike a driver's license, where individuals do not have the choice with whom they will interact on the road, consumers generally can choose with whom they obtain a regulated service.

The focus of this chapter is to analyze the impact of occupational licensing on the supply of practitioners and estimate the impact of licensing on earnings. The structure of the chapter initially provides a brief theoretical background of the impact of changes in the supply of licensed occupations on both state-regulated and unregulated occupations. Next, a case study of two occupations—dentists and physicians—is examined to show how changes in the supply of practitioners can impact earnings. A review of the literature is provided on the impact of changes in the supply of regulated occupations on earnings. The rest of the chapter is devoted to examining how licensing impacts earnings for large groups of licensed occupations using data from the census and the National Longitudinal Survey of Youth (NLSY), as well as statutory and pass rate data from the states. The concluding section focuses on comparisons between both regulated and unregulated occupations, and how tougher licensing laws and administrative procedures impact earnings.

THEORETICAL BACKGROUND

A basic microeconomic analysis of licensing argues that regulation restricts entry into one occupation and can create an oversupply in others (see Filer, Hammermesh, and Rees 1994). Although licensing may impose costs to consumers as shown in Chapter 3, the examination in this chapter focuses mainly on supply implications of licensing. Figure 4.1 illustrates the potential effects of licensing. Panel A shows the implementation of licensing on the supply of labor for occupation 1 shifting to the left from S to S^1 with a fixed demand for labor D_L. The consequences for occupation 1 are a reduction in employment from E to E^1 and an increase in earnings from W to W^1. If the newly regulated occupations contain a large number of workers, then there is also an effect on the unlicensed occupations. In Panel B, workers from Panel A who are now unable to legally do work in occupation 1 shift the supply curve for occupation 2 to the right from S^* to S^{**}. The implications for occupation 2 are an increase in the employment of unregulated workers from E^* to E^{**} and a reduction in the wage of individuals in the occupation from W^* to W^{**}.

The implications of the model presented in Figure 4.1 suggest that licensing not only has the effect of raising wages and reducing employment in the regulated occupation but also reducing wages and increasing employment in the unregulated occupation. The consequences of occupational licensing are not only within the regulated occupation but also can serve to dampen wage benefits for workers in other occupations. Therefore, comparisons of the labor market effects of licensing also need to examine the effects on unlicensed occupations. Empirically analyzing the full effects of licensing should examine similar unlicensed occupations as the counterfactual for the labor market consequences of regulation. The next section gives an example of the impact of labor supply and earnings by comparing two highly skilled licensed occupations where general regulation and other conditions in the market for health care may have contributed to supply shifts.

LICENSE TO DRILL: DIFFERENCES IN EARNINGS OF DENTISTS AND PHYSICIANS

Although the fictional James Bond may have had a more expansive license to "kill" in numerous novels and movies, the American Dental Association's ability to restrict supply in part through licensing for dentists has contributed to a lucrative and growing source of income for individuals in this profession. A classic and often cited study completed

Figure 4.1 Impact of Implementing Occupational Licensing in the Regulated and Unregulated Sectors

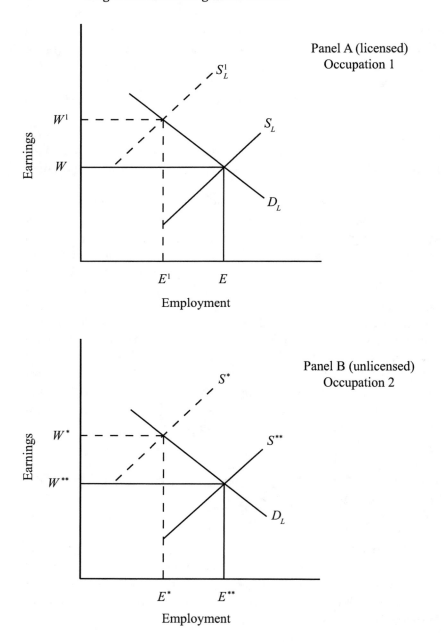

through the National Bureau of Economic Research by economists Milton Friedman and Simon Kuznets estimates that the 33 percent difference in the higher earnings of physicians relative to dentists was due to more than just a year's difference between the requirements to become a doctor versus a dentist (Friedman and Kuznets 1945). They estimate that the difference in earnings between doctors and dentists should be about 17 percent based on human capital and other observable factors, but that the additional 16 percent residual gap is in large part a consequence of physicians' relative ability to restrict labor supply. Milton Friedman's book *Capitalism and Freedom* argues that physicians were able to obtain substantial earnings gains over dentists during the 1920s and 1930s because they were able to limit the number of new student enrollments in medical school (Friedman 1962a). However, more recently there has been a reversal of these trends.

There was a more than 23 percent growth in the number of new physicians from 1990 to 2000 (Scopp 2003). In contrast, there was no growth in the total number of dentists over the same period. Dental school enrollment increased by only 1 percent per year during the 1990s, and the number of dentists in the United States remained constant over the decade as a result of retirements and individuals leaving the occupation (American Dental Education Association 2004; U.S. Census Bureau 2000).

Why did the number of dentists remain constant during the 1990s? In large part this stable supply was a part of the larger boom and bust cycle in the production of dentists during the last century. During the 1960s federal policies were established to fund an increase in the number of health care specialists, including dentists. Dental enrollments increased substantially over the next two decades (Field 1995). This funding for expansion resulted in an increase in the number of dentists in the United States both through the creation of new dental schools and increases in the enrollment capacity of existing schools. With a recession of the early 1980s, there was a decline in the demand for dentists and in their earnings (Field 1995). During this decline, the American Dental Association and state licensing boards attempted to "regulate" the number of new dentists, resulting in a reduction in the supply of new dentists (Field 1995). A major producer of dental graduates, the University of Minnesota, reduced its entering class by almost 30 percent from the early 1980s to 2000.

Another element of the lack of increase in the number of dentists was the closing of several large dental schools such as those at Northwestern University, Washington University, and Georgetown University. Administrators at Northwestern University stated that a large part of their decision to close their dental school was that the cost to operate expensive clinics as required by the state and recommended by the American Dental Association was prohibitive (Hagen 2001). In contrast, physician-training clinics generally were subcontracted to local hospitals and were not part of the administrative costs of operating the medical school. It is unclear why these schools did not raise tuition for dental education to cover the higher costs of training for dentists relative to doctors. With the decline in the number of dental schools and a reduction in new entrants at the remaining ones, as well as the normal attrition and retirements, the absolute number of dentists in the United States remained stable from 1990 to 2000, even though the overall population increased.

Did the decline in the number of dentists and the growth in the number of physicians have any impact on the relative earnings of individuals in these occupations? Figure 4.2 gives the relative hourly earnings of dentists and doctors age 20 to 65 from 1990 and 2000 from the 5 percent sample from the U.S census.[1] In 1990 physicians' hourly earnings were 98 percent that of dentists. However, doctors earned more than dentists for almost every age beyond 36. In part this is because younger physicians were still earning training wages as interns and residents in their early 30s, whereas dentists were usually already in full-time practice. The growth in the number of physicians relative to the number of dentists during the decade of the 1990s is one likely explanation for this reversal in relative earnings in these two professions. As Figure 4.2 shows, by 2000 dentists' hourly earnings, which include bonuses and returns to private sector practices, were above those of doctors for almost all age groups except for individuals over the age of 63, when dentists often retired but physicians' earnings continued to rise. Data from this figure show that physicians were making only 82 percent as much as dentists by 2000, with the earnings of dentists above those of physicians at most age levels. The relative decline in dentists' labor supply, as well as other changes in the way dental services are provided, which included state regulations for having dentists on site when hygienists do their work, contributed to increases. In addition, dentists provided more

Figure 4.2 Hourly Earnings of Physicians and Dentists, by Age, 1990 and 2000 ($)

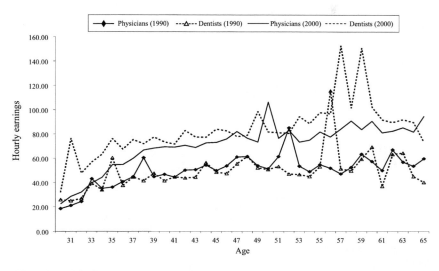

SOURCE: U.S. Census Bureau (2000).

"fee for service" relative to doctors whose fees were often constrained by HMOs and Medicare. The next sections give information on statistical studies that examine the impacts of occupational regulation on earnings and labor supply.

STUDIES ON THE IMPACT OF LICENSING

The area of occupational regulation that has received the most attention by researchers has been the question of the extent to which licensing restricts entry, as well as the impact of these restrictions on earnings and the supply of individuals in these occupations. Table 4.1 summarizes the results of many of the major studies on this topic. Panel A presents the key findings of studies that focus on the earnings of teachers, physicians, dentists, lawyers, barbers, and cosmetologists. The results show considerable variation in the effects of regulation. For the higher-education and higher-income occupations working mainly in

Table 4.1 Studies on Earnings and Labor Supply Effects of Licensing in the United States

Authors	Occupation	Findings
A. Earnings effects		
White (1980)	Registered nurses	Licensing has no impact on pay.
Kleiner and Petree (1988)	Teachers	Licensing has no impact on teacher pay.
Anderson et al. (2000)	Physicians and alternative medicine practitioners	Physicians in states with stricter regulations on alternative medicine earn significantly higher incomes.
Kleiner (2000)	Dentists, lawyers, barbers, and cosmetologists	Earnings are higher for licensed occupations that require more education and training relative to comparable unlicensed occupations.
Kleiner and Kudrle (2000)	Dentists	Practitioners in the most regulated states earn 12 percent more than those in the least regulated states.
Tenn (2001)	Lawyers	Low rates of interstate in-migration and outmigration, a common effect of licensing, is associated with high wages.
Angrist and Guryan (2003)	Teachers	State-mandated teacher testing increases teacher salaries.
B. Supply effects: including employment and migration effects		
Thornton and Weintraub (1979)	Barbers	Licensing of barbers has little impact on the number of individuals entering the trade.
Boulier (1980)	Dentists	Lack of national reciprocity restricts migration, resulting in a net loss in consumer welfare.
Pashigian (1980)	Eight licensed occupations, with an emphasis on lawyers	The most pronounced effect of licensing is the reduced interstate mobility of members in licensed occupations. Restrictions on the use of reciprocity reduce interstate mobility still more.

Table 4.1 (continued)

Authors	Occupation	Findings
White (1980)	Registered nurses	Licensing has no impact on employment levels.
Carroll and Gaston (1981)	Electricians, dentists, plumbers, real estate agents, optometrists, sanitarians, and veterinarians	Licensing lowers the total stock of practitioners.
Kleiner, Gay, and Greene (1982)	Accountants, architects, engineers, lawyers, dentists, pharmacists, physicians, surveyors, insurance agents, real estate agents, registered nurses, practical nurses, barbers, and cosmetologists	Licensing acts as a barrier to mobility, causing a misallocation of labor resources across states. A system of universal endorsement would increase gross inmigration of the identified practitioners by over 60 percent.

the quasi-private sector, like physicians, dentists, and lawyers, licensing appears to have large effects through either limiting entry or restricting movement to the state. However, for other occupations such as teachers, nurses, and cosmetologists, the impact of licensing on earnings is murky, with some studies finding small effects and others finding none. Panel B gives the employment and state migration effects of licensing. Again the results vary by occupation. For barbers and nurses the impact of regulation on labor supply is small. However, for other occupations, licensing's impact on employment in a state by limiting the movement of practitioners across states or counties can be substantial. This migration effect appears to be of sufficient magnitude to result in a geographic misallocation of interstate occupational resources and perhaps has a long-term effect on the geographic allocation of human capital.

Similar to the variation of the impact of unionism on relative wages across occupations and industries, there are also differences in the impact of licensing on earnings largely based on the characteristics of the occupation (Lewis 1986). To the extent that a pattern exists, it appears that occupations that deal directly with customers or patients or are allowed to work independent of other licensed occupations are most likely to receive the largest economic benefits from occupational licensing. For example, dentists, in part through a reduction in the supply of new entrants into the occupation from 1990 to 2000, received larger pay increases than any other major regulated occupation. Lawyers, through restrictions on interstate mobility, also have been able to obtain economic benefits for practitioners (Tenn 2001). Physicians, by limiting the supply of alternative medicine providers, have been able to enhance the earnings of the members of their occupation (Anderson et al. 2000). On the other hand, occupations such as teachers and nurses have not been able to significantly enhance the earnings in their profession through licensing, perhaps as a consequence of the market structure of their employment relationship. Unlike doctors, dentists, and lawyers, nurses and teachers work primarily for large institutions like hospitals or school boards. The work of nurses and dental hygienists requires the oversight of doctors and dentists. Hospital and school administrators have incentives to reduce costs within their organization and likely will put pressure on legislatures to ease licensing restrictions to ensure an ample supply of practitioners. Moreover, for nurses and teachers the primary mode of determining wages, hours, and other terms and conditions of employment is through labor relations and collective bargaining with an employer.

An occupation that has been at the forefront of the growth of tougher licensing is public school teachers. This is a relatively new phenomenon in comparison with the other occupations in our analysis, with most of the states beginning to engage in tougher licensing standards during the 1980s. Moreover, licensing with state-administered exams only became the norm during the 1990s. Although some analysis has suggested that the recent regulation of teachers has had little quality effect as measured by human capital or student achievement, there has been little analysis of the impact of regulation relative to similar occupations (Angrist and Guryan 2003).

EARNINGS OF LICENSED VERSUS UNLICENSED OCCUPATIONS

One way to analyze the impact of licensing on regulated occupations is to compare the earnings of the licensed occupation relative to similar occupations that are not regulated. George Stigler, in his often-cited paper covering the theory of regulation, devoted a significant amount of his analysis to occupational licensing and found that licensed occupations earned more than unregulated ones using data from the 1960 census (Stigler 1971). His estimates show that unregulated occupations earned one-third less than regulated ones, and that unregulated occupations earned 12 percent less than partially regulated ones. Unfortunately, there were no control variables to account for differences in human capital or regional differences. In order to examine this issue in greater detail, I compare the earnings of persons who are accountants, cosmetologists, dentists, physicians, lawyers, and teachers to individuals who work in unlicensed occupations and are listed in the census within the same one-digit job family. This implies that they have similar job requirements. The focus of the analysis is to examine the counterfactual of what would be the impact on the earnings of individuals in an occupation if that occupation ceased to be regulated while maintaining other general education and experience-related factors.

Appendix C presents a listing of the licensed and unlicensed comparison occupations in our sample by census two- and three-digit occupation code. The comparison occupations have similar education and work skill sets as the regulated ones. Based solely on observable general human capital factors, these occupations are similar.

Table 4.2 gives the regression estimates of the impact of licensing on earnings using different statistical specifications of the earnings equation for these listed occupations. In self-reporting on census forms, some individuals overstate their occupational affiliations, especially in unlicensed occupations. For example, chemical technicians, who do not have bachelor's degrees, may answer that they are chemists on the census form. Therefore, the analysis is presented both for individuals who claimed to be in the occupation and for individuals who identified themselves as being in the occupation and stated that they also had the minimum level of education generally required for the work. These alternative specifications give the results of a truncated sample with only those individuals who meet the minimum expected level of education for that occupation.

The expectation is that there are characteristics of individuals who chose an occupation that would cause them to select one occupation over another. Consequently, the table gives results of estimates of the impact of licensing with the general human capital variables and the inclusion of a self-selection correction variable, which adjusts the estimates for potential omitted variables,[2] which may result in persons choosing a regulated versus an unregulated occupation (Heckman 1979). In all these specifications licensing is estimated as a dummy variable, with one denoting a licensed occupation and zero an unlicensed one. Accountants are included in this analysis since CPAs are licensed in all states, but most accountants do not have a CPA. Column one shows the impact of licensing when basic human capital variables are controlled for, as well as self-selection issues for entering a licensed occupation in this regression model.[3] These estimates include all who claimed to be in the occupation in the census in 1990 and 2000, a sample size of more than one million. The results show that being in a licensed occupation enhances the hourly earnings of the regulated occupations by about 10.0 percent. The coefficient value on licensing is precisely estimated and is statistically significant at the 99 percent confidence level using group-corrected for the standard errors. In the second column estimates are

Table 4.2 Estimates of the Aggregate Impact of Licensing on Hourly Wages for Selected Occupations in 1990 and 2000

Variables	Total census sample	Limited by minimum education
Licensed	0.10	0.12
	(0.02)	(0.06)
Age	0.05	0.07
	(0.02)	(0.03)
AgeSQ	0.00	0.00
	(0.00)	(0.00)
Female	−0.37	−0.39
	(0.12)	(0.13)
White	−0.15	−0.19
	(0.11)	(0.18)
UScitizen	0.03	0.25
	(0.04)	(0.14)
Ln(pGsp)[a]	0.64	0.79
	(0.18)	(0.25)
Ln(Population)	−0.07	−0.10
	(0.08)	(0.09)
Year2000	−0.15	−0.14
	(0.10)	(0.13)
Education	0.12	
	(0.02)	
Mills ratio	−0.03	−0.04
	(0.06)	(0.15)
Constant	3.63	5.88
	(1.98)	(2.34)
Number of observations	1,044,141	740,227
R^2	0.37	0.15

NOTE: Group corrected standard errors are in parentheses. Occupations include personnel and labor relations managers; accountants and auditors; purchasing agents and buyers, farm products; computer systems analysts and scientists; actuaries; statisticians; mathematical scientists, n.e.c.; chemists, except biochemists; teachers, prekindergarten and kindergarten; teachers, elementary school; teachers, special education; librarians; economists; sociologists; social workers; clergy; lawyers; biological and life scientists; physicians; dentists; veterinarians; optometrists; podiatrists; registered nurses; pharmacists; postsecondary teachers, subject n.s.; judges; public relations specialists; dental hygienists; licensed practical nurses; bartenders; waiters and waitresses; maids and housemen; barbers; hairdressers and cosmetologists.
[a] pGsp is per capita gross state product.

developed from a truncated sample of only those individuals who have completed general education at the minimum level associated with the occupation. For example, the minimal level of education for teachers is a four-year college degree, whereas graduate education is required for attorneys and physicians. The sample size using minimum education cutoff criteria by occupation is still large, with more than 740,000 individuals in the sample. Again, this coefficient value is large, showing a 12 percent impact, yet it is measured with somewhat less precision and is statistically significant at the 5 percent confidence level.[4] The results from Table 4.2 show that being in a licensed occupation has a moderately large impact on the hourly earnings of the individuals in the occupation, with magnitudes similar to those obtained by being in a union (Lewis 1986). With these reduced-form estimates, it is difficult to know if the impacts on earnings are a result of supply restrictions generally promoted by professional associations that represent these licensed occupations or the additional general, specific, or continuing education requirements that enhance the productivity of the individuals in these regulated occupations.

Another methodological approach that uses occupations analyzed in Table 4.2 is to find the impact of licensing on earnings for those individuals who switched from being in an unlicensed occupation to a regulated one and vice versa (Mincer 1986). Most of the estimates presented in this chapter refer to the average impact of regulation, but this type of analysis could be interpreted as the marginal impact of changing to a regulated occupation from an unregulated one. In order to do this, I examine individuals in the NLSY who switched from an unlicensed occupation to a licensed one for years 1984 to 2000. In addition, I examine individuals who went from a regulated occupation to an unregulated one. The expectation is that individuals who change their jobs or occupations do so in an attempt to make an economic gain. This research approach attempts to control for individual human capital characteristics as well as other unobservables that cannot be captured within a regression framework. The results of these estimates are presented in Table 4.3. They show that full-time workers, who are not in school and change their occupations, have large percentage increases in their wages in their first year of employment. For example, switching to an unlicensed occupation from a licensed one results in a 26 percent increase in earnings, but the switch from an unlicensed occupation to a

Table 4.3 Percentage Change in Hourly Wages after Switching Occupations Using NLSY, 1984–2000[a]

	Median percentage wage change		
	From licensed to nonlicensed (1)	From nonlicensed to licensed (2)	Percent gain due to licensing
Persons who change occupations at least once	26% ($n = 99$)	43% ($n = 119$)	17%

[a] Estimates include only full-time workers who are not in school, and are adjusted by the wage deflator by year.

licensed one is associated with a 43 percent increase in hourly earnings. If the general switching of occupations estimate is 26 percent, then the overall licensing impact is 17 percent in the first period following the change.[5] The larger estimate can be interpreted as the marginal effect of moving into a licensed occupation similar to findings of physicians who became licensed in Israel relative to those who did not (Kugler and Sauer 2005). Additional estimates for "new" lawyers in the United States find that tougher licensing raises their starting earnings by almost 37 percent (Pagliero 2004). In summary, these approaches indicate that the gains in changing to a licensed occupation are larger relative to changers who move in the other direction. These results indicate that the marginal effect of becoming licensed is larger than the average impacts shown in cross-section estimates.

Although the estimates provided in Table 4.2 give overall results of the impact of licensing on earnings for an aggregate group of occupations, they do not provide results for individual occupations relative to a relevant comparison group. In order to provide more detailed results of the impact of licensing, Table 4.4 gives estimates by regulated occupation along with its related unlicensed comparison. The estimates continue to use census data and information on the overall regulatory status of the occupation. The table provides analysis for the following licensed occupations: physicians, dentists, teachers, lawyers, and cosmetologists, along with the occupations that have similar educational and skill requirements but are not licensed. Accountants are not included in this portion of the analysis since we are examining only occupations where all or most of the individuals are assumed to hold a current

Table 4.4 Parameter Estimates of the Impact of Licensing on Hourly Wages Relative to Similar Unlicensed Occupations[a]

Occupation	Parameter estimates
Physicians	
Biological and life scientists	0.407
Dentists	
Biological and life scientists	0.643
Teachers[b]	
Public relations specialists	0.000
Lawyers	
Economists	0.048
Sociologists	0.454
Cosmetologists	
Bartenders	0.042
Waiters and waitresses	0.063
Maids and housemen	0.112

[a] Estimates include individuals with minimum level of education and the controls listed in Table 4.2.
[b] The sample for teachers is limited by state average starting salary in the year before the 2000 census year.

or provisional license in order to work.[6] The specifications presented are for the truncated sample of individuals who met the minimum education requirements. These results are consistent with those in Table 4.2 and show that licensing usually has positive and statistically significant impacts on hourly earnings. Nevertheless, there are substantial variations in the magnitudes of the results, with dentists showing the largest licensing impact on earnings relative to its comparison occupation, while teachers have the smallest coefficient values. Perhaps public sector administrators and school boards are able to lobby legislatures to obtain exemptions from strict regulations and thereby increase the supply, which modifies the ability of public sector unions to obtain significant pay increases for their members. Clearly, the choice of the comparison occupations may also influence the results, and I am not able to find whether supply shifts in the regulated occupation or the unregulated occupation are contributing to the earnings impacts of regulation.

These results suggest that occupations that have a market structure that serves individual clients like physicians and dentists seem to gain more from licensing than individuals who work in occupations whose primary employer is a school board or corporate or nonprofit entity (Wheelan 1999). There is some evidence that large employers who are organized can lobby state legislatures to obtain more relaxed licensing provisions or exemptions from licensing laws that allow them to do the work of licensed practitioners. In the case of teachers and administrators, this means allowing provisional teaching certificates for teachers. For example, in Texas almost 20 percent of the teachers in the public schools had provisional certificates rather than licenses, which allows school boards to hire them as teachers with the understanding that they must eventually become licensed.

For teachers, the effects of licensing are virtually zero on the log of hourly earnings based on the specification, and are small for cosmetologists. The rationale for regulation having a counterintuitive effect may be twofold. First, state regulators or state occupation or labor force planners, who are often members of the occupation, may not have chosen the optimal supply of persons in the occupation in order to maximize earnings. For them, restricting entry even further may have resulted in a greater growth of earnings in the occupation. Second, even though restricting supply may be in the best interests of the occupation, state legislators may not allow certain statutes to be passed, or they may monitor licensing regulatory bodies that are responsible for setting pass rates or otherwise serving as a "port of entry" into the occupation. Consequently, occupations that are similar but do not limit supply through state regulations may have similar earnings.

Although Tables 4.2 through 4.4 present statistical evidence of the effect of being licensed on earnings, they do not answer the question of what would have been the earnings of the regulated occupation if they had the characteristics of the unregulated occupation. A way to think about this "experiment" is to assume that there was a "trading places" of the regulated and unregulated individuals. To further show the earnings effect, I present an earnings gap analysis that estimates what licensed persons would have earned if they had been in an unregulated occupation. This approach builds on the analysis of what would have been the earnings outcome if all the measured characteristics of one group were given to the other group, except licensing. For example, using this approach assumes that the market rewards individuals differently for each year of schooling, age, or experience based on whether the individual was licensed. In order to do the statistical analysis of developing a counterfactual for this issue, a decomposition analysis is specified.[7] This procedure does a statistical "trading places" using the regulated and the unregulated occupations. Since there is relatively little mobility between the two groups, the assumption of noncompeting groups for these two occupations is plausible. For each person in the regulated occupation, the model predicts what would have been the earnings of the individual if they were not regulated at each position of the earnings distribution.[8] Therefore, the expectation is that the earnings in the unregulated occupation would be to the left of the actual distribution of the regulated occupation, depicting what would have been the distribution of earnings if the individual in the licensed occupation became unlicensed.

A caveat to the decomposition analysis is that individuals who have greater unobservable ability characteristics, such as better social skills or aptitudes, may choose to enter a licensed occupation where the economic returns are higher than ones that require similar abilities but are unregulated. Since there is a large queue of persons wishing to enter these regulated occupations, part of the returns to individuals in licensed occupations may be the higher-quality labor market skills of persons in regulated occupations that consumers perceive as higher-quality services (see Chapter 3). Another reason for the higher earnings of licensed occupations lies in the regulated occupations' ability to restrict supply and thereby increase the earnings of its members. However, there may be labor market mistakes by the occupational association through overestimating the demand for the service and consequently increasing the number of practitioners. The increase in supply of practitioners could be accomplished through lobbying by occupational associations, such as the American Medical Association or the American Dental Association, to increase new entrants into the occupation or by relaxing immigration requirements. The process could occur over time through recommendations to professional schools and state legislatures to expand entering classes or change mobility constraints across political boundaries. In addition, regulatory planners, licensing board members who are responsible for administering the exam, and the organizations representing the professions who seek tougher state statutes may allow too many persons into the occupation, thereby reducing earnings in the occupation relative to unregulated labor markets, whose earnings are dominated through the supply of individuals in the occupation and demand conditions. Similar to some industries where union wages are lower than nonunion wages, there may be occupations where regulated wages are below those in similar unlicensed occupations.

The statistical approach for the decomposition analysis uses a semi-parametric estimate of the impact of earnings for each group along each stage of the earnings distribution. The analysis allows for a graphical representation of the total distribution of individuals in both the regulated and unregulated occupations. In this case the graph shows all hourly income earners of the licensed occupation superimposed on a figure that shows how much the individuals would have made if they were unregulated. This approach shows the impact of licensing at each point along the hourly earnings distribution. The coefficients are derived from the estimates in Tables 4.2 and 4.4, where the basic method estimates two standard log wage regressions using the variables in these tables, one for licensed and one for unlicensed. Predicted wages for licensed individuals are generated from each regression, and the difference is the value of earnings for each occupation if that occupation were not regulated for each point along the earnings distribution.[9] The main advantage of this methodology is that the entire wage distribution is analyzed, allowing the licensing factor to have different effects at different points along the distribution. Thus, unlike traditional decomposition analysis, which usually presents differences at the mean of a distribution or quartile regressions, the decomposition technique is unique in that it uses semi-parametric estimates that allow one to decompose the changes in the entire log wage distribution. The semi-parametric decomposition method also allows one to gauge how much of the total discrepancy between two wage distributions can be explained by this type of occupational regulation.

The drawbacks of this approach are the assumptions of no spillovers between the licensed and unlicensed occupations. Another drawback of the approach is that the estimation and interpretation of the results can be difficult. In addition, the method provides point estimates of the wage distributions, but there are no standard errors, and rigorous hypothesis testing has not been developed, outside of using bootstrapping techniques with simulations (Budd and McCall 2001).

Figure 4.3 shows graphical representations of the decomposition analysis for five licensed occupations—physicians, dentists, lawyers, teachers, and cosmetologists—relative to the comparison group of unlicensed occupations by the states, which includes biological and life scientists, economists, sociologists, public relations specialists, bartenders, waiters and waitresses, and maids and housemen. The figures for the semi-parametric results are consistent with the regression estimates presented in Tables 4.2 and 4.4. These figures show that regulation raises earnings along most segments of the earnings curve for all of the occupations examined, both relative to their comparison occupation (i.e., the dashed lines) and in comparison to what they would have earned if the occupation were not regulated (i.e., the dotted lines). The results are consistent with the regression estimates in the previous tables in the chapter, showing that licensing raises earnings relative to occupations that were unregulated.

The semi-parametric approach shows more clearly and in detail the results of the differences along each part of the estimated wage distribution in Figure 4.3. However, the size of the regulation impact varies by both the licensed and unlicensed occupation used in the comparisons. For example, the spread for dentists relative to its comparison occupation is much larger than for teachers in comparison to its "opportunity cost" occupation. Using all of the statistical approaches in the chapter thus far shows consistent results; namely, being in a licensed occupation has a positive effect on earnings relative to similar unregulated occupations and relative to being unlicensed. Nevertheless, this analysis does not examine whether licensing impacts occupations that are licensed in some states but not in others. Consequently, I now turn the analysis to the impact of statutes and administrative procedures on the earnings of practitioners who are not regulated in many states.

PARTIAL STATE REGULATION OF OCCUPATIONS

For most of the occupations regulated in the United States, there is licensing in some states but not in others. One issue is whether being in a state that regulates an occupation through licensing has any impact on the earnings of the individuals relative to states that do not regulate

Figure 4.3 Semi-Parametric Estimates of the Impact of Licensing on Hourly Wages

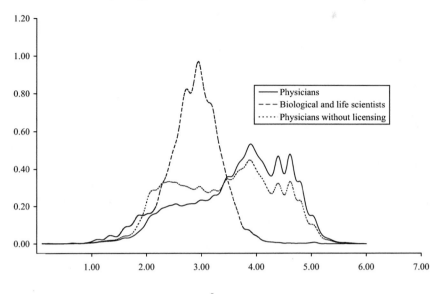

Log wage

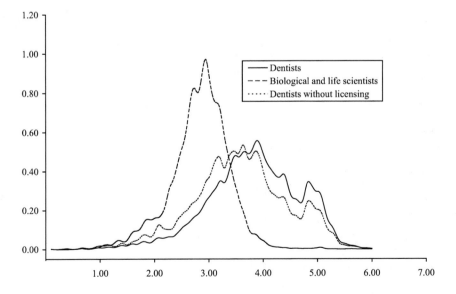

Log wage

Figure 4.3 (continued)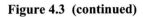

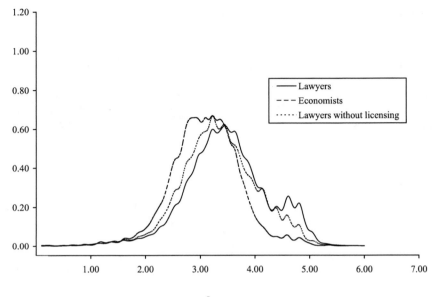

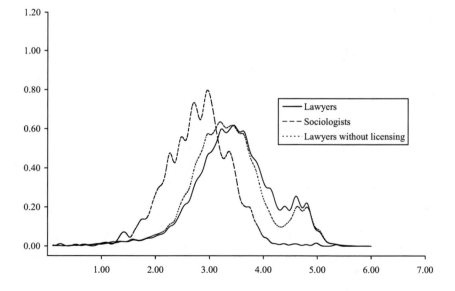

Figure 4.3 (continued)

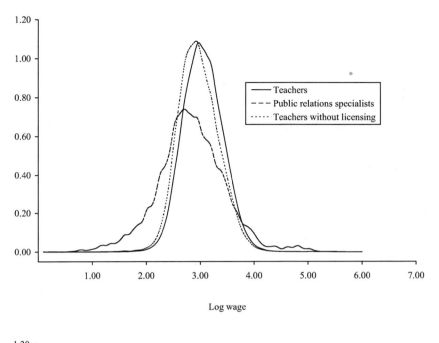

Log wage

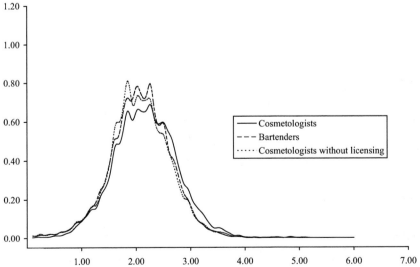

Log wage

Figure 4.3 (continued)

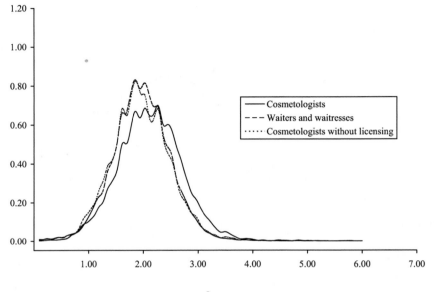

Log wage

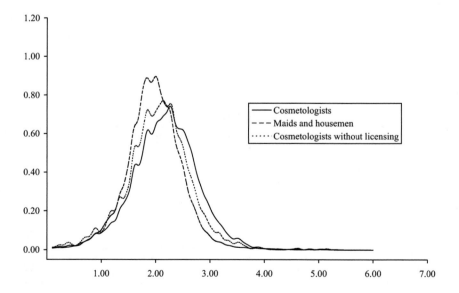

Log wage

the occupation. Table 4.5 shows the impact of being in a state that licenses an occupation relative to ones that do not, using similar human capital and state level statistical control variables as presented in Table 4.2. These estimates are for more than 2.7 million partially regulated workers from the 2000 census, and they show that licensing has a statistically significant impact on hourly earnings of more than 4 percent. This estimate is smaller than the ones presented in Table 4.2, which compared licensed occupations relative to unlicensed ones. Part of the smaller impact may be due to spillover of higher wages from regulated states to unregulated ones. Organizations representing the occupations who operate in regulated states may apply an administered wage across state lines to maintain wage contours for the profession (Dunlop 1993), possibly resulting in the narrowing of wage differences across states for the same occupations.

These results support the view that licensing enhances the earnings of the individuals in regulated occupations, but they do not indicate whether this increase in earnings is a consequence of the restriction of supply of regulated practitioners, enhanced human capital gathered as a consequence of higher educational standards, or enhanced reputation capital which is perceived by consumers as existing in a regulated occupation (discussed in Chapter 3). Nevertheless, these results provide additional evidence that states that, by choosing to regulate an occupation, it may also drive up the hourly earnings of the practitioners in that state. This analysis does not answer the question of whether already universally licensed occupations can get higher earnings by making those regulations tougher through statutory provisions or through manipulating administrative procedures like the pass rate.

SMALL DIFFERENCES IN LICENSING RULES THAT MAY MATTER

Two major types of institutional licensing variables often impact the earnings of licensed occupations. First, statutory factors such as general and specific levels of education required to become licensed tend to vary by state. These include measures of good moral character, citizenship, residency in the state for specific periods of time, and rec-

Table 4.5 Impacts of Partial State Licensing on Hourly Wages for Regulated Occupations

Variables	Cross-section regression[a]
Licensed in state	0.04
	(0.01)
Age	0.08
	(0.00)
AgeSquared	0.00
	(0.00)
Female	−0.30
	(0.01)
White	0.08
	(0.01)
UScitizen	0.08
	(0.02)
$Ln(pGsp)$[b]	0.51
	(0.05)
Ln(Population)	0.03
	(0.01)
Education	0.08
	(0.00)
Constant	1.15
	(0.24)
Number of observations	2,756,892
R^2	0.25

NOTE: Group-corrected standard errors are in parentheses.
[a] Estimates are for 2000.
[b] pGsp is per capita gross state product.

ommendations from current practitioners. States can vary in the stringency with which they each set the requirements for practicing in an occupation. Second, states can set their own pass rates for individuals to be granted entry into the occupation within the state.

A further set of requirements is established for individuals who attempt to move to a state from elsewhere. These requirements include similar general and specific statutory education requirements as those entering the occupation but with several exceptions. Oftentimes this means retaking certain specific parts of the original licensing exam to enter the occupation. As an alternative to retaking the state exam, some states require working with a licensed practitioner to ensure that the out-of-state applicant follows current state procedures. Often, requirements are waived if the individual has worked in the occupation for a lengthy period of time, such as five years. Reciprocity agreements mean that states can establish virtual "treaties" with other states to allow them to accept each other's licensed practitioners without additional education or tests. The statutes and agreements with other political entities vary from accepting any applicant from another state who has a valid license at one end of a continuum to endorsement or acceptance of applicants if they meet the entry requirements in force at the time of initial licensure or currently in force within the state, to reciprocity only with states that have signed agreements (Kleiner, Gay, and Greene 1982; Tenn 2001). States vary a great deal by occupation in how they allow licensed practitioners from other states or countries to enter and work within their political jurisdiction.

To quantify the statutory factors that impact licensing, a composite index is used to obtain a quantitative value of the relative restrictiveness of each state's licensing provisions. The indices chosen were a summated rating scale and a Rasch index. The Rasch index uses a Guttman-type ordering of each of the statutory values. The seeming ordering of the statutes of licensing practices suggests a ranking of states by their licensing activity: those with high levels of statutory rigor or intensity for the toughest statute would have the highest ranks, those with lower levels of statutory intensity for that feature would be next, followed by those with high levels of statutory intensity for the second most restrictive law, and so on. One latent variable model that fits these data well is Rasch-type models (Wang 1997).[10] This index is developed so that it estimates the effect of regulation on both earnings and supply using a logit form to estimate the latent ability (statutory progressiveness) of respondents (states). An even simpler way to summarize the data for the statutes is to form a summated rating by adding together the levels attached to different responses (Bartholomew 1996). With a 0/1 coding for the presence or absence of a practice, a state with five statutes gets a 5, while one with three statutes gets a 3 scale, and so on. The model uses both Rasch and summated ratings to estimate the value of the statutory provisions of the legal measures. The estimates show a similar distribution of states by the Rasch and the summated rating measure of licensing. The two summary statistics give similar scalings with a simple correlation of around 0.6. The Rasch estimates are used in the empirical analysis, but the results hold for the summated ratings scale as well. They also hold for factor analytic methods that form a single factor eigenvalue for these legal measures.

Using the summated rating approach adds up the values of each of the statutory requirements for licensure to form one measure of the restrictiveness of entry into the occupation. Based on the relative restrictiveness of the state statutes, the states were then divided into high, medium, and low regulation states for each occupation. Another measure of restrictiveness was the pass rate in the state. The assumption is that the lower the pass rate, the more restrictive the state is regarding its licensing administrative procedures. In other studies pass rates are estimated to be the most significant regulatory factor in the determination of earnings (Kleiner and Kudrle 2000). Both the statutory regulations and the pass rate on the state-administered exam serve to restrict entry and create potential barriers to working in an occupation.

Table 4.6 shows results of estimates of the impact of statutory index values and pass rates on the hourly earnings for cosmetologists, dentists, lawyers, physicians, and teachers.[11] There are two sets of control variables. One group holds constant for human capital factors such as race, gender, education, age, age-squared, and citizenship. The second set of control variables accounts for demand factors in the state that may impact earnings, including population and per-capita gross state product in the state.[12] Column one presents the impact of tougher licensing using a Rasch index measure of regulation, and it includes a dummy variable control for the year of the observation for those occupations for which there is data for 1990 and 2000. The second column presents the impact of the statutes on earnings for the upper one-third of the states in terms of their relative restrictiveness using the summated rating scale, and they also include a dummy variable control for the year of the observation. The last column shows the impact of the pass rate on earnings of the practitioners. The results show that tougher licensing statutes had positive and significant impacts on the level of earnings of practitioners for two of the five occupations, namely for cosmetologists and physicians. However, for the pass rates, there was no statistical impact on the earnings of the practitioners for either lawyers or cosmetologists. Similarly, changes in the statutory provisions over the decade do not have an impact on the change in earnings of these licensed practitioners. Pos-

Table 4.6 Estimates of the Impact of Tougher State Regulations on Hourly Wages[a]

Occupation	Regulations (Rasch)	Regulations (high)	Pass rate
Cosmetologists	0.00	0.08	0.00
	(0.01)	(0.04)	(0.00)
Sample size	6,374	6,374	3,078[c]
Dentists[b]	0.01	0.02	
	(0.02)	(0.04)	
Sample size	6,567	6,567	
Lawyers	0.00	−0.02	0.00
	(0.01)	(0.02)	(0.00)
Sample size	65,599	65,599	65,599
Physicians	0.00	0.03	
	(0.00)	(0.01)	
Sample size	53,033	53,033	
Teachers	−0.01	−0.03	
	(0.02)	(0.03)	
Sample size	196,313	196,313	

NOTE: Group-corrected standard errors are in parentheses.
[a] With the following controls: Age, Age squared, Gender, Education, Race, UScitizen, Ln(per capita Gross state product), Ln(Population), and Year 2000.
[b] Using only the census year 2000 sample.
[c] Using only the census year 1990 sample.

sibly these estimates were due to the changes in the provisions that were small and occurred late in the decade and therefore were likely to have only modest effects. Or, perhaps there was not impact because these legal provisions paled in comparison to administrative factors such as the pass rate.

CONCLUSIONS

This chapter examines the impact of being licensed and of variations in state statutes on earnings for several regulated occupations, with a focus on the supply-side impacts. A basic labor market model shows that a reduction in the supply of licensed practitioners increases earnings of regulated workers but may lower the earnings of individuals in the unregulated occupations. An example is shown for the changes in the earnings of physicians and dentists. The supply of physicians increased during the 1990s, whereas the number of dentists remained constant. Dental earnings increased relative to those of physicians at almost every age of their working lives.

To develop more general results, this chapter examines the impact of being in a licensed occupation on the hourly earnings of universally regulated occupations relative to similar unlicensed counterparts using data from the 1990 and 2000 census. For the occupations examined, being in a licensed occupation appears to increase earnings between 10 to 12 percent, which is at the lower bound of the impact of other labor market institutions, such as unions. For individuals whose occupation is licensed in some states and not in others, the impact of being licensed is much smaller (4 percent). The chapter also examines five universally licensed occupations (doctors, dentists, teachers, lawyers, and cosmetologists) and compares them to similar occupations that are unlicensed. The estimates show that, with the exception of teachers, all have some positive earnings effects relative to their selected "opportunity cost" occupations. To provide more precision to the results, the analysis shows semi-parametric estimates of the impact of being in a licensed versus unlicensed occupation and the effect of licensing along all points of the earnings distribution using the specifications of the estimates and simulation methods. Finally, this chapter examines the impact of variations in state licensing laws and pass rates on earnings. The results show the impacts are small—on the order of 3 to 8 percent for doctors and cosmetologists in relatively highly regulated states, and they are zero for teachers and lawyers.

Licensing increases the economic status of most practitioners. Policymakers need to examine whether these increases are a result of increased quality caused by greater training and higher-quality services, or a consequence of restricting competition through the limiting of entry into the occupations, or both. The evidence provided in Chapter 3 suggests that the benefits of licensing are mainly for individuals who have insurance benefits or are relatively wealthy. Consequently, policy options like certification with retesting, which is the case with driver's licenses, may be sufficient to result in the quality benefits without the potential negative effects of restricting competition. The next chapter examines in greater detail the trends in licensing laws and administrative procedures, and how these laws impact consumers, workers, practitioners, and the public.

Notes

1. An issue using census data for high-income occupations is that the results are "top-coded," which means that individuals above certain income levels receive the value between $75,000 and $175,000 from 1980 to 2000 depending on the census year. The estimates below of doctors and dentists for census years show the following percentage of individuals were top-coded from 1980, 1990, and 2000. The rate of dentist to physician top-coding in 2000 relative to 1990 biases the estimates in Figure 4.2 toward dentists gaining even more income relative to physicians from 1990 to 2000.

	Dentists %	Physicians %	Top-coded limit ($)
1980	13.32	18.25	75,000
1990	12.50	23.40	140,000
2000	20.01	26.14	175,000

2. Estimates without the self-selection variable showed similar significant licensing impacts ranging from 8 to 15 percent.
3. The instrumental variable used to identify the equation for the inverse Mills ratio used to implement the selection variable was the nonlabor income in the household minus the individual's income, with dummies for the relationship to the head of the household. See Neuman and Oaxaca (2003) for a similar specification.
4. Estimates using separate male and female equation models showed similar impacts of licensing on earnings.
5. Using a fixed-effects research design shows the switching occupation impact as 34.5 percent, and under this assumption, the licensing impact on earnings drops to 8.5 percent.
6. There were 1,733,220 persons who stated that they were accountants in the 2000 census, and there were 577,000 persons who are licensed CPAs in the United

States (American Institute of Certified Public Accountants 2004). Nevertheless, licensing laws govern the behavior of individuals doing accounting tasks. Consequently, accountants were not included in this section of the analysis.

7. A basic mathematical presentation of the form of the decomposition analysis can be stated as follows:

$$W_l = \alpha_l + \Sigma\beta_{jlw}X_{jlw} \text{ and } W_{nl} = \alpha_{nl} + \Sigma\beta_{jnlw}X_{jnlw},$$

where W is earnings and X is a vector including all observable factors such as education and experience. The subscripts nl signify nonregulated occupations, and l signifies a regulated occupation. Using the standard algebra of the decomposition analysis, the simplified equation becomes:

$$\overline{W_l} - \overline{W_{nl}} = \Sigma[\beta_{jlw}(\overline{X_{jlw}} - \overline{X_{jnlw}})] + [(\alpha_l - \alpha_{nl}) + \Sigma(\beta_{jlw} - \beta_{jnlw})\overline{X_{jnlw}}]$$

(Filer, Hammermesh, and Rees 1994).

8. Probabilities that different characteristics appear in regulated and nonregulated occupations are calculated from logit models and incorporated into kernel density estimation so that counterfactual distributions can be constructed. With these counterfactuals, one can analyze, for example, what the wage distribution would have looked like in 2000 if the individual were unlicensed and thereby assess the relative importance of that factor in explaining the observed changes in wage outcomes due to that factor (DiNardo, Fortin, and Lemieux 1996).

9. The procedure for generating the semi-parametric estimates is a nonparametric kernel density estimation. The kernel function is simply a weighting function so that observations closer to the point of interest are weighted more heavily than observations farther away from this point. For graphical display, the density function estimate is calculated for a number of equally spaced evaluation points. In the analysis that is presented, the observations of interest are individuals' log real wages, using a Gaussian kernel function with 200 evaluation points and a bandwidth of 0.05. A major advantage of this methodology is that we can examine the entire wage distribution in contrast to standard summary measures such as a discrimination coefficient or a Gini coefficient.

10. Rasch-type models have the following properties: they are unidimensional, require discrete observations, require statistical independence, and can be estimated using maximum likelihood techniques (Andrich 1988). If the latent variables are continuous, then the standard technique is factor analysis using the largest positive Eigenvalue.

11. These estimates are in a reduced form that includes both supply and demand variables that impact earnings of practitioners in these occupations.

12. Each of the state-level controls has standard errors adjusted for group bias in the regression estimates.

5

State Regulatory Policies and the Economy-wide Impacts of Licensing

In a clash between state licensing regulators and a conservative branch of the Pennsylvania Amish, one of its members was fined $1,000 for practicing dentistry without a license. For the last thirteen years, Crist Zook has been pulling the teeth of his Amish neighbors. While he did not get a university education he read up on Dentistry, acquired instruments and found a source of prescription painkiller Novocain. Zook was always available and had a good safety record.

—*Sunday Patriot News*, Harrisburg, Pennsylvania, August 13, 1995

This newspaper report shows the potential clash of state licensing policies and religious practices. As more occupations seek to become licensed or to increase statutory requirements and job control, confrontations are likely to occur between groups seeking nonlicensed services and laws restricting those services. To illustrate, dental hygienists seek to practice without the supervision of a licensed dentist, but dentists have lobbied extensively for restraints on the ability of hygienists to practice alone or even to whiten teeth without the presence of a licensed dentist (Simms 2004). Moreover, dental hygienists are seeking legal restraints on what type of work nonlicensed dental assistants can do within a dental office since they often do the tasks of regulated hygienists (Hallman 2004). The growth of licensing has resulted in numerous conflicts not only among licensed and nonlicensed workers, but among occupations that are licensed and do similar work for consumers, such as dentists and hygienists. With the greater use of Internet transactions for regulated products and services, there has been a growing controversy over state licensing regulations and federal concerns about restrictions on interstate commerce (Kleiner 2002). As many occupations seek to become regulated, this phenomenon continues to require additional ways of looking at this traditional issue with new data and analysis.

The stated objectives of licensing laws are to increase competence and reduce negligence of practitioners (Office of the Legislative Auditor, State of Minnesota 1999). The goal of this chapter is to present the basic facts on state licensing and the direction of regulatory legislation and administrative practices for certain universally regulated occupations, as well as to provide a rationale for and estimates of the potential societal gains or losses from licensing. The first section details some basic facts on state-by-state licensing. The next section examines the changes in the statutory requirements and administrative procedures to practice for accountants, attorneys, cosmetologists, dentists, and teachers in large states and nationally. The concluding section presents a method of estimating impacts of licensing on wages and employment as well as providing an assessment of potential losses to society. The summary to the chapter discusses the rationale for licensing in advanced industrial societies and suggests how looking at other nations' regulation of occupations may provide useful insights into these questions.

STATE DATA ON THE NUMBER OF LICENSED OCCUPATIONS AND THE NUMBER OF WORKERS

The difference between a good and bad haircut is two days.

—James Ragan, Department of Economics, Kansas State University, March 12, 2004[1]

The above quote suggests that quality issues for licensed barbers are relatively small and that licensing benefits to consumers of barbering services also are likely to be small, yet barbering is licensed in all 50 states. Licensing in the United States is state-by-state rather than national, as in other countries such as France. To fully understand the impact of licensing, it is important to know about the basic facts and trends of this form of regulation. As a consequence of this structure of regulation in the United States, there is much variation in the number of occupations regulated and the percentage of the workforce in each state that must have a state-sanctioned permit to work. One reason for this disparity across states may be the ability of the advocates for the occupation to obtain regulation for the members of the occupation (Rottenberg 1980; Wheelan 1999). Issues like the extent of political organizational commitment and the financial contributions to political parties by the profession may have important impacts on whether the occupation can convince members of the state legislature that they should be licensed. Often the number of persons in the occupation in the state can help determine whether the members of the occupation are successful in obtaining state licensing. If the policy of a national profession is to have its occupation universally licensed, then the state chapters often make this topic their main political goal. This was the case when respiratory therapists sought to obtain licensing status in all states (Wheelan 2005).

Table 5.1 shows the number of occupations that are licensed, by state, using data from the Department of Labor's Labor Market Information Survey, as stated at its Web site: http://www.acinet.org/acinet/default.asp. These data were matched with occupations listed in the 2000 census. If the occupation given by the state enumeration was not listed in the 2000 census, it was dropped from the listing. As a result, the values in Table 5.1 understate the actual number of occupations that are regulated in each state.[2] The listing of licensed occupations by state shows much variation in the number of regulated occupations. To illustrate, California and Connecticut license more than 150 occupations, but Kansas regulates fewer than 50. The median state, Nevada, regulates about 88 occupations at the state level. The states that have the 5 highest numbers of licensed occupations average about 146 regulated occupations, but the bottom five states average about 53 licensed occupations. Therefore, the most regulated states license almost three times the number of the least regulated ones. The data from this table only provide information from the state level, but counties and cities often impose additional requirements or have their own additional listing of occupations that are licensed within their political jurisdiction.

One of the important political questions in occupational regulation is why states like Iowa regulate 82 occupations but neighboring Kansas only licenses 47. A deeper examination of the labor force composition and the political environment of the two states and the political awareness of the occupational associations may provide some insights into the reasons for the variation in licensing coverage for these two states. Figure 5.1 maps the percentage of the workforce covered by licensing

**Table 5.1 Number of Occupations Licensed, by State, and Their Relative
           Rank, 2000**

State	Number of licensed occupations	Rank
California	178	1
Connecticut	154	2
Arkansas	140	3
Maine	139	4
Michigan	118	5
Wisconsin	117	6
Tennessee	114	7
North Carolina	113	8
New Hampshire	112	9
Rhode Island	112	10
New Jersey	109	11
Oregon	108	12
Ohio	107	13
Florida	106	14
Vermont	106	15
Massachusetts	105	16
New Mexico	101	17
Idaho	99	18
Alaska	96	19
Illinois	94	20
Minnesota	94	21
Nebraska	94	22
Oklahoma	93	23
Washington	92	24
Maryland	89	25
South Dakota	89	26
Nevada	88	27
Kentucky	87	28
Georgia	83	29
Indiana	83	30
Iowa	82	31
Louisiana	81	32
Delaware	80	33

Table 5.1 (continued)

State	Number of licensed occupations	Rank
Virginia	80	34
Utah	79	35
Montana	78	36
New York	73	37
West Virginia	72	38
Texas	71	39
Wyoming	67	40
Alabama	64	41
North Dakota	63	42
Colorado	62	43
Missouri	60	44
Hawaii	60	45
Mississippi	55	46
South Carolina	55	47
Arizona	54	48
Pennsylvania	53	49
Kansas	47	50

SOURCE: America's Career InfoNet (2005).

Figure 5.1 Percent of Workforce Licensed, by State, 2000

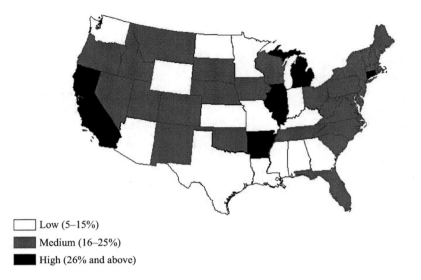

☐ Low (5–15%)

▦ Medium (16–25%)

■ High (26% and above)

NOTE: Alaska and Hawaii are in the "Medium" category.
SOURCE: America's Career InfoNet (2005); U.S. Census Bureau (2000).

laws, by state, using categories of low, medium, and high. This figure shows that the most regulated states are on the East and West Coasts, and in the heavily industrialized states in the Midwest. The only major exception is the state of Arkansas, where many occupations became regulated during the 1980s.

WORKFORCE COVERAGE OF LICENSED OCCUPATIONS BY STATE

Although knowing the number of occupations that are licensed is useful as a proxy for the status of occupational regulation in a state, it does not give the coverage of the workforce that is directly subject to state regulation. Table 5.2 shows the percentage of the employed workforce that is covered by licensing laws in each state. There is a comparable amount of variation in the percentage of the workforce that

Table 5.2 Percent of Workers Covered by Licensing, 2000

State	Licensed	Total	Percent
Alabama	263,800	2,015,620	13.09
Alaska	75,320	330,420	22.80
Arizona	296,140	2,399,600	12.34
Arkansas	345,360	1,209,260	28.56
California	4,802,460	15,820,040	30.36
Colorado	523,000	2,338,540	22.36
Connecticut	528,560	1,757,260	30.08
Delaware	78,780	399,120	19.74
Florida	1,666,140	7,501,560	22.21
Georgia	555,580	4,023,880	13.81
Hawaii	113,700	598,920	18.98
Idaho	120,200	621,800	19.33
Illinois	1,697,540	6,165,300	27.53
Indiana	367,120	3,066,380	11.97
Iowa	234,480	1,525,080	15.37
Kansas	161,860	1,360,260	11.90
Kentucky	223,920	1,868,560	11.98
Louisiana	274,080	1,969,200	13.92
Maine	137,520	657,000	20.93
Maryland	567,260	2,780,060	20.40
Massachusetts	737,360	3,339,880	22.08
Michigan	1,368,620	4,841,900	28.27
Minnesota	352,860	2,667,700	13.23
Mississippi	74,980	1,228,500	6.10
Missouri	344,760	2,763,020	12.48
Montana	92,300	457,900	20.16
Nebraska	203,040	885,400	22.93
Nevada	198,460	1,022,100	19.42
New Hampshire	165,820	676,720	24.50
New Jersey	777,260	4,219,380	18.42
New Mexico	193,340	824,940	23.44
New York	1,430,980	9,061,380	15.79
North Carolina	943,340	4,017,060	23.48
North Dakota	40,500	328,860	12.32
Ohio	1,153,480	5,647,700	20.42
Oklahoma	306,700	1,630,940	18.81

Table 5.2 (continued)

State	Licensed	Total	Percent
Oregon	327,200	1,716,180	19.07
Pennsylvania	956,120	5,967,660	16.02
Rhode Island	129,920	535,920	24.24
South Carolina	325,960	1,910,720	17.06
South Dakota	72,320	380,420	19.01
Tennessee	590,260	2,754,020	21.43
Texas	1,350,160	9,883,880	13.66
Utah	186,480	1,093,480	17.05
Vermont	79,480	332,280	23.92
Virginia	625,500	3,684,300	16.98
Washington	360,700	2,988,680	12.07
West Virginia	142,220	767,060	18.54
Wisconsin	694,920	2,847,320	24.41
Wyoming	28,620	254,620	11.24
Total	27,286,480	137,137,880	19.90

SOURCE: America's Career InfoNet (2005); U.S. Census Bureau (2000).

is licensed by states as for the variation in the number of occupations regulated by the states.

Although the national average for the percentage of the workforce that is licensed is 19.9 percent in 2000, there is much variation in the percentage of the workforce that is regulated. For example, California licensing coverage is about 30.4 percent of its workforce, but Mississippi regulates only 6.1 percent of its workforce through licensing. The ratio of licensed employment coverage to total employment of the top five states (average is 28.9 percent) to the bottom five states (average is 10.6) is more than 2.7 times as large, which is similar to the variation in the results shown in Table 5.1. Generally, states with high population density or heavily industrialized states such as California, Connecticut, and Illinois tend to have higher levels of occupational licensing than more rural or lower-income states like Mississippi or Wyoming.

Larger and more urbanized states seem to be more likely to have stronger organizations that represent occupations, and they can obtain regulation for their members as a form of "rent capture" for their occupations. Moreover, urbanized states may want to obtain the benefits of credentialing that licensing provides, since many of the commercial interactions that occur in more densely populated areas are impersonal transactions with little repeat business, and this may require more regulation as a form of consumer protection. Consumers of the service and legislators also may see the regulation of these services through licensing as a method of quality control through the elimination of "lemons from the market" (Akerlof 1970).

TRENDS IN THE REGULATION OF
LICENSED OCCUPATIONS

There has been a consistent upward trend in the growth of the number of laws or administrative procedures that regulate occupations (Kleiner and Gordon 1996). However, for some occupations that have been regulated for a long time, the trend has been toward fewer restrictions. On the other hand, newly regulated occupations generally have seen an increase in the level of statutory regulations over time. Figure 5.2 summarizes these trends for several universally licensed occupations over a 20-year period, using an index value for accountants, attorneys, cosmetologists, dentists, and teachers. The statutory regulations examined vary by occupations but generally include a residency requirement, reciprocity with other states or the endorsement of qualifications from other states, minimum score requirements in order to retake other sections of the exam, years of experience required to take or receive a license, and the number of continuing education requirements needed to maintain the license.

Accountants have increased requirements for entry by the states as shown in Figure 5.2. Unlike many of the other occupations that are licensed in all states, individuals can perform many accounting functions for pay without having a license. However, to provide official information on the financial state of a company requires a certified public accountant (CPA) license. These laws mandate that individuals meet state requirements that include age, residency, general education, and accounting-specific information. Reciprocity with other states is given if the individual has 5 or 10 years of CPA experience. One of the major changes in the licensing of CPAs has been the requirement that individuals must have 150 hours of relevant university-level classes, effectively increasing requirements for the license by one year.

For attorneys, the plot in the figure measures an index of the state requirements for the following qualifications: residency, accepts attorneys who are admitted to the bar in other states, uses the multistate bar exam, requires graduation from an American Bar Association–approved school, and requires that law students register with the State Board of Bar Examiners. The requirements for cosmetologists contain fewer general and specific education requirements and are less rigorous, but the summary still measures whether the state requires minimum levels of general education, specific education, an apprenticeship in lieu of education, whether there is reciprocity, and if the state has a minimum passing score. Even though the requirements are lower than for the other occupations, barbers and cosmetologists generally require at least nine months of schooling and apprenticeships that last approximately a year and a half. The trends in the figure also measure these requirements. Teacher index requirements for licensure include whether a professional education degree is required, a second stage certificate or a master's degree, whether an exam is required to enter a teacher preparation program, reciprocity, and if a major is required for secondary

**Figure 5.2 Time-Series Statute Index for Five Universally
Licensed Occupations**

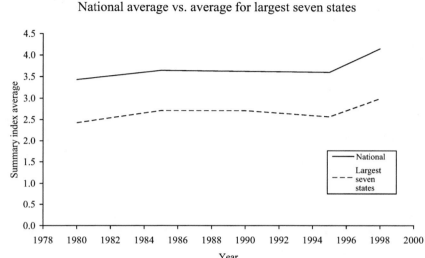

Accountants

National average vs. average for largest seven states

NOTE: Summary index includes minimum scores applicant must have on failed
sections in order to retain conditional approval and years of experience required to
1) receive a CPA certificate, 2) sit for CPA exam, or 3) receive permit or license to
practice, 150 hours continuing education/graduate education, and semester hours of
accounting classes. Largest seven states by population are California, Florida, Illinois,
New York, Ohio, Pennsylvania, and Texas.
SOURCE: *Digest of State Accountancy Laws and State Board Regulations,* various
years.

Figure 5.2 (continued)

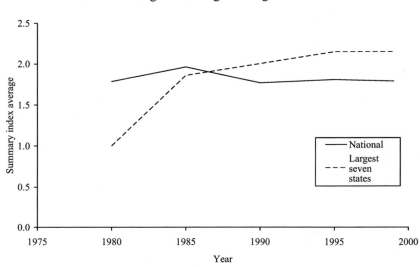

Attorneys

National average vs. average for largest seven states

NOTE: Summary index includes residency, whether a state has a provision for admission on motion, whether a state accepts out-of-state Multi-state Bar Examination scores, whether an applicant must have received a J.D. from an American Bar Association-approved school to qualify for admission on motion, and whether a state requires law students to register with the State Board of Bar Examiners. Largest seven states are California, Florida, Illinois, New York, Ohio, Pennsylvania, and Texas.

SOURCE: *Comprehensive Guide to Bar Admission Requirements,* various years, and *A Review of Legal Education in the United States, Law Schools, and Bar Admission Requirements,* various years.

Figure 5.2 (continued)

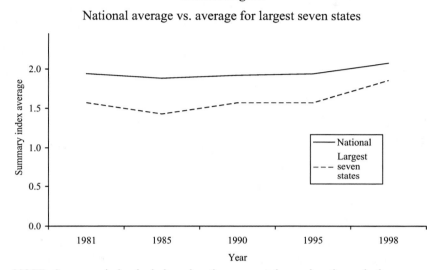

Cosmetologists

National average vs. average for largest seven states

NOTE: Summary index includes education, cosmetology education, whether an apprenticeship is permitted in lieu of education, reciprocity, and minimum passing score. Largest seven states are California, Florida, Illinois, New York, Ohio, Pennsylvania, and Texas.

SOURCE: *Milady's Guide to Cosmetology Licensing,* various years, and author's compilation of state statutes, various years.

Figure 5.2 (continued)

Dentists

National average vs. average for largest seven states

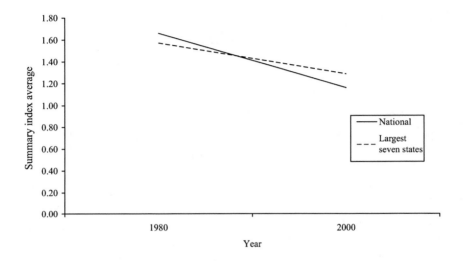

NOTE: Summary index includes education and reciprocity/endorsement. Largest seven states are California, Florida, Illinois, Ohio, New York, Pennsylvania, and Texas.
SOURCE: *Facts about States for the Dentist Seeking a Location,* various years, and author's complilation of state statutes, various years.

Figure 5.2 (continued)

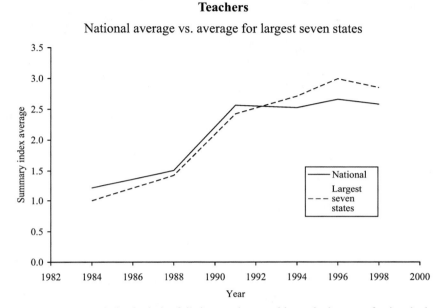

Teachers

National average vs. average for largest seven states

NOTE: Summary index includes full-time student teaching, whether a professional education degree is required or not accepted, whether a state that requires a second-stage
certificate requires a master's degree or 5th year for that certificate, whether an exam
is required to enter a teacher preparation program or obtain initial certification, reciprocity, and whether secondary school teachers require major/minor in subject taught.
Largest seven states are California, Florida, Illinois, New York, Ohio, Pennsylvania,
and Texas.
SOURCE: *National Association of State Directors of Teacher Education and Certification Manual,* various years; Eissenberg and Rudner (1988); and Childs and Rudner
(1990).

school teachers. For dentists, the requirements are that the individuals have an undergraduate degree plus at least 48 months of dental school training. Figure 5.3 shows national pass rates, which are collected by the national associations, for CPA accountants and cosmetologists during the 1980s and 1990s.

The results in both Figures 5.2 and 5.3 show much variation in the changes in the stringency of licensing requirements over time for these five occupations. For example, dentists' legal requirements have declined, but there has been little overall change in the toughness of the statutes for cosmetologists and attorneys. On the other hand, accountant and teacher requirements have increased. The largest jump in the toughness of licensing requirements occurred for teachers. The average state only had one of the five key licensing provisions in 1984, but the average state had increased its requirements to between 2.5 and 3 of the licensing provisions by 2000. This largely reflected the push toward state-level exams and the greater difficulty in moving across states by teachers, much of which was promoted by teacher unions. In contrast, the number of licensing restrictions fell for dentists, largely reflecting the move to multistate testing and the greater acceptance of out-of-state dentists over this time period. The trends in licensing in the largest seven states by population generally reflect the trends in the laws in other smaller states as shown in the figures. Either through the influence of the lobbying organizations that represent the occupations or through efforts at standardization across states during this period, there were similar trends across these five occupations in the kinds of legal provisions that were enacted across the United States in large and small states.

LICENSING AND ECONOMIC LOSSES TO SOCIETY

Have these state regulations on occupations impacted the economy? The previous chapters showed that, for most licensed occupations, there is a wage premium that ranges from 4 percent for partially licensed occupations to 12 percent for occupations that are licensed relative to their nonlicensed counterparts. Based on the results presented in Chapter 3, licensing is associated with an increase in the price of the regulated service in most cases. Although there may be gains to the individuals in the

Figure 5.3 National Pass Rates for Accountants and Cosmetologists

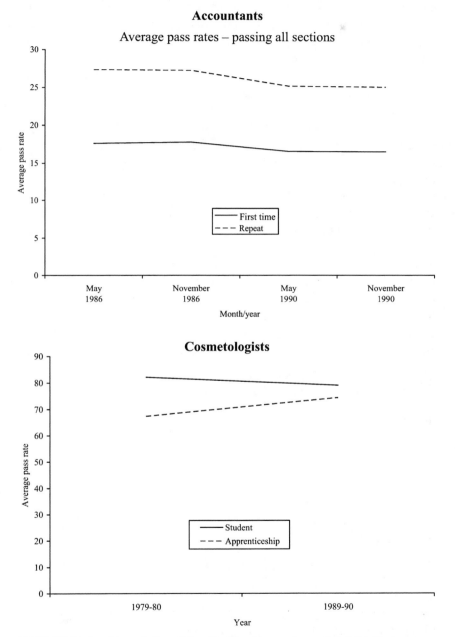

SOURCE: National Association of State Boards of Accountancy, Candidate Performance on the Uniform CPA Examination (national data compiled since 1982); and *Milady's Guide to Cosmetology Licensing,* various years.

regulated occupation through higher wages, there also may be losses to society through lost output. When an occupation becomes regulated, wages and prices usually go up (Rottenberg 1980). If there is a standard downward sloping demand curve, then increases in the price of the service may result in both a reallocation of income from consumers to the purveyor of the service and the loss of the services to society through lower employment and fewer services.

Figure 5.4 shows the basic underlying modeling approach to the assumption that licensing results in potential "dead-weight losses" to society (Blanchflower and Freeman 1992). Before the implementation of licensing, wages are W and employment is at E. If licensing is implemented across all states for the occupation or if licensing is adopted in a state, then wages increase to W' and employment is reduced to E'. If the service wage and price go up, consumers purchase less of the service. As a result, the white rectangle area between W and W' under the curve goes to the practitioners, but the shaded triangle area is lost output due to occupational regulation. Within this standard economic model of regulation, there are gains to the practitioners through higher wages. However, some who may have been in the occupation may suffer wage loss as a consequence of licensing, as consumers find substitutes or engage in "do-it-yourself" remedies. Furthermore, there are likely to be

Figure 5.4 Potential Lost Service Output as a Result of the Implementation of Occupational Licensing

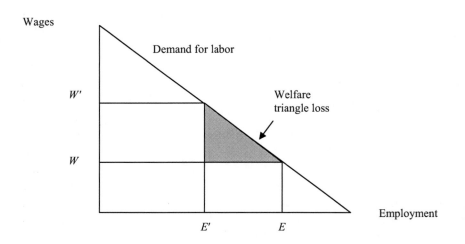

overall losses to society in the form of lost output, which is part of the "welfare triangle loss" in Figure 5.4. This loss is the difference between the increased earnings of the practitioners due to licensing and lost employment multiplied by their forgone earnings in this figure. An outcome of this potential loss is that licensing results in fewer choices and higher prices for consumers. The full effect of licensing on employment may be mitigated by regulation, which increases the quality of the service provided. Nevertheless, the impact of licensing would result in lost employment and service output to society.

A simple method of calculating potential lost output as a consequence of licensing can be estimated using the approach in Figure 5.4 and related statistical information in this book. For example, there is little evidence that overall quality or output is increased as a consequence of licensing. Although for certain groups, for example, those with higher incomes or generous insurance coverage, tougher licensing does result in better services. In Chapter 4 the estimates show that individuals in licensed occupations earn about 10 to 12 percent more than their nonlicensed counterparts. Furthermore, if licensed occupations comprise about 20 percent of the total workforce, licensing drives up economy-wide costs to consumers by about 2 to 2.4 percent relative to a labor market where no one was licensed. Compared to total wage income in the United States of $5.8 trillion in 2000, the estimated reallocation of earnings from consumers to licensed practitioners is between $116 billion and $139 billion in 2000 dollars using this approach. Using economy-wide average or medium estimates derived by Hammermesh (1993) of the elasticity of labor demand of 0.3, the "dead-weight loss" to society of licensing is between $34.8 and $41.7 billion per year (Hammermesh 1993).[3] This value can also serve as a background for what might be an alternative to licensing, such as the certification of occupations, which allows individuals to practice without government sanctions but without the ability to use the occupational title. This example of the magnitudes of the effects of licensing under these assumptions suggests that this form of labor market regulation has moderate quantitative impacts on the costs and quantity of services. However, the benefits of licensing, such as signaling quality and providing some perceived protection to potentially large downside consumer losses by eliminating the least qualified potential practitioners, may be worth the added cost of licensing to society by giving consumers perceived protection against the worst-case outcome scenario (Kahneman and Thaler 1991).

CONCLUSIONS

Licensing in the United States has taken many varied forms, based in large part on the occupation that is being regulated. Some occupations, such as cosmetologists, have relatively few requirements for working. Others, including dentists, have long training periods with many state-level requirements for entry into this profession. However, a larger source of variation in occupational regulation occurs among the states. Some states, like Mississippi, regulate relatively few occupations that include less than 10 percent of its workforce, but others, such as California, license up to 178 occupations that include more than 30 percent of its workforce. Generally, more urbanized states license higher percentages of their workforces. Trends in licensing also vary a great deal. For example, the number and intensity of the requirements to become a teacher have greatly increased. Twenty-seven states required applicants to pass a standardized test to be licensed to teach in public schools in 1987, but the number had grown to 41 by 1999 (Angrist and Guryan 2003). Other occupations, such as dentistry, have reduced their requirements over the past 20 years. There does not seem to be a large difference in the kinds of statutes—or in the trends in their adoption—in large states relative to smaller ones.

An economic approach to examining the impact of licensing shows that it results in a movement up the demand curve for labor, which reduces employment and causes a potential economic loss to society. Using estimates from the U.S. economy and licensing data gathered from this book, licensing results in a "dead-weight" loss to the U.S. economy of approximately $34.8 to $41.7 billion per year in 2000 relative to a labor market without licensing. This should be balanced against the benefits of licensing, such as signaling quality and providing some downside protection to consumers as a consequence of the poor quality of the least qualified potential practitioners.

Since licensing has been among the fastest growing labor market institutions in the United States over the past half century, more data have become available to track its growth and impact. The patterns of growth have been similar to other patterns in the labor market, such as industrialization and unionization. In those states that are heavily urbanized, licensing has generally become more pervasive. One reason for this phenomenon is the greater organization of the professions and their ability to put pressure on legislatures to seek licensure or, as in the case of teachers, increase the requirements for entering the occupation. Nevertheless, there is a need for signals of quality in the labor market, which an institution like licensing provides to consumers of regulated services. Two key policy questions are whether certification would reduce the economic losses that licensing has through its monopoly effects on restricting entry, and whether certification is a politically viable alternative to the tougher state-mandated alternative of licensing.

Are the licensing impacts in the United States unique, or do other democratic industrialized nations also find the need to license their workforces in a similar manner? The next chapter examines and compares the licensing requirements in the largest countries in the EU with the United States. This comparison is useful in examining the extent to which licensing and its impacts are unique to the United States or determining whether this analysis and its policy implications can be expanded to other industrialized nations.

Notes

1. I want to thank Jim Ragan for this quote, which he attributed to his Uncle Virgil (following a haircut from said uncle).
2. An example of the understatement of the estimates in Table 5.1 is the state of Minnesota, which listed 188 licensed occupations in 1999, but they included sports licenses and obscure occupations, such as crop hail adjuster and weather modifier, for which no census categories are listed (Office of the Legislative Auditor, State of Minnesota 1999).
3. Other simulated estimates using values of personal consumption expenditures as the basis of the reallocation estimates produced similar outcomes for the reallocation effects and "dead-weight loss" results.

6

Comparing Licensing in the United States and the European Union

Millions of Europeans, from bartenders to soccer stars, have to deal with what might be called the certification complex—a requirement that they be certified to pursue their jobs in a time-consuming process dating back to 19th-century apprenticeships. Economists say it is a big reason behind Europe's high unemployment and lagging productivity.

—John Miller, *Wall Street Journal,* August 16, 2004

As the above quote suggests, the regulation of occupations is perceived to be a major factor in the lack of efficiency in the labor market and a contributor to lagging productivity and high unemployment in Europe. Is this the case, and do the European methods of regulating occupations have different outcomes from those in the United States? The focus of this chapter is to present the basic data on and analysis of the labor market impact of licensing in the three largest EU countries: France, Germany, and the UK. Prior to 2003, these nations comprised more than 51 percent of the EU workforce (Statistical Office of the European Communities 2004). This analysis will be used to compare the impacts of licensing in the EU relative to the United States.

For licensed occupations in both the United States and the EU, the government is able to control who gets to work and how the task is done. However, licensing follows divergent paths in both cases and results in varied labor market outcomes. In most EU countries, licensing is national and, for most professions, there is no licensing exam beyond passing the classes in order to graduate from an accredited school.[1] However, the regulatory trade-off in the EU is that, for most occupations, practitioners are regulated more heavily after they are working. Unlike the generally market-oriented focus of U.S. occupational licensing laws following entry, the level of fees, method of payment (e.g., contingency or hourly), and advertising are all regulated by the government in the EU (Garoupa 2004). Consequently, there is likely to be much greater

variation in earnings of licensed practitioners in the United States because of fewer post-entry regulations of licensed practitioners. In addition, earnings of licensed individuals in the EU are likely to mimic the
overall earnings distribution in the EU, with relatively high minimum
earnings and lower upper bounds for workers. Generous social safety
nets and relatively higher taxes in the EU result in a much narrower
wage and earnings distribution than in the United States (Filer, Hammermesh, and Rees 1994). Moreover, for most occupations in medical
specialties, such as physicians and dentists, a large proportion of practitioners work for the government or are limited by government pay
scales. Finally, for many of the regulated occupations, subsidies by EU
governments for education in medical and other specialties often result
in a justification for regulations that limit earnings. The remainder of
this chapter documents the regulations that licensed practitioners work
under and estimates the impact of licensing on earnings in comparison
to unregulated occupations in the three largest countries in the EU.

OCCUPATIONAL REGULATION IN THE EU

The nations in the EU have only recently focused public policy
attention on the economic and labor market consequences of occupational licensing (Paterson, Fink, and Ogus 2003). Occupational regulation across countries has been divided into two general categories:
structural regulation and behavioral regulation. Examples of structural regulation include entry restrictions and the granting of exclusive
rights to perform certain services. These types of restrictions would
likely be promulgated by the organizations associated with the occupation and would be a form of public interest regulation. Examples of
behavioral regulation include rules regarding the level or structure of
professional fees and limitations on advertising (Commission of the
European Communities 2004). For this type of regulation the "social
planner" would likely restrict the upper bound for prices, but the occupational association may view this as acceptable if the lowest price
that could be charged were sufficiently high to satisfy the majority of
the members of the occupation. This process may be similar to unions
setting the minimum negotiated wage for a large number of employees

at a sufficiently high level, but this policy may come at the price of a truncated upper wage (Freeman and Medoff 1984).

This type of regulation in the EU impacts both the price and the level of employment. Regulation in the United States occurs through the restriction of entry or employment, but the price or wage can be set by the market for the service. Restrictions in the EU occur both through regulations on entry and through limitations on prices. Consequently, the restrictions are likely to manifest themselves in wait time and shortages for the service. Table 6.1 shows attitudinal data for users of health services for the UK and United States, and it shows that perceptions of wait times and shortages for appointments and the time to see health professionals are substantially higher in the UK relative to the United States (Commonwealth Fund 2002). This table shows patient attitudes

Table 6.1 Survey Perceptions of "Wait Time" and Shortages for UK and U.S. Patients

Most frequently cited problems	UK	U.S.
High cost of health care	6	48
Shortages	33	5
Waiting times	39	3
Need for increased number of health professionals	15	2
Having to wait for an appointment, long waiting times for type of care	75	40

NOTE: The International Health Policy Survey (Commonwealth Fund 2002) consisted of interviews with adults with health problems in each of five countries: Australia, Canada, New Zealand, the UK, and the United States. To identify these adults, the survey screened initial random samples of adults 18 or older who met at least one of the four following criteria: reported their health as fair or poor; had serious illness, injury, or disability that required intensive medical care in the past two years; had major surgery in the last two years; or had been hospitalized for something other than a normal, uncomplicated delivery of a baby. These questions resulted in a final sample of 750 or more "sicker adults" in each country who were eligible to participate in the full survey (AUS, 844; CAN, 750; NZ, 750; UK, 750; U.S., 755). This final survey sample represents one-fourth to one-third of the adults initially contacted. These sicker adults are among the most intensive users of the health care system and are particularly vulnerable to variations in quality and outcomes of care. Harris Interactive, Inc. and country affiliates conducted the interviews by telephone between March and May 2002.

toward the wait time for medical services, which are the most heavily regulated occupations in both the United States and the EU. On the other hand, complaints about price are much greater in the United States (48 percent) relative to the UK (6 percent). Unfortunately, the survey results are not available for Germany or France, but the available results show that complaints about a shortage of health professionals are 15 percent in the UK relative to 2 percent in the United States. Overall the data in this table show that, at least for the UK, putting greater constraints on both employment and prices can lead to shortages, which manifest themselves in longer waiting times for patients.

Unlike the Department of Labor and Census Bureau data in the United States, which allow for the tabulation of an estimate of the number of regulated occupations, there is no central agency that gathers data on the number of persons who are licensed by country in the EU. It is therefore difficult to estimate the number of occupations licensed in the EU or the density level of licensing as a percentage of the workforce in Europe. Consequently, my examination of licensing in the EU will be focused on a country-by-country basis with an emphasis on specific occupations rather than the relatively large number of occupations that were examined for the United States. Nevertheless, estimates are provided of the overall impact of licensing for a group of regulated occupations across the UK, France, and Germany, and these are likely to be representative of the larger body of licensed occupations in these nations.

The focus on the port of entry for joining a licensed occupation is on the educational establishments rather than passing licensing exams following the completion of schooling. An example of the method for becoming licensed in the EU is provided through the licensing process for dentists in the UK. To work as a dentist in the UK, one must obtain a license from the General Dental Council (GDC) and be put "on the register" (Jetha 2002). A candidate must graduate from a dental school accredited by the GDC or be subject to EU regulations on mobility of professionals across countries. If an individual is from a non-UK or non-EU dental school, a licensing exam is required to be listed on the GDC registry. Requirements for becoming a dentist include being in dental school at least five years, which is up from four years. In contrast, U.S. dentists must obtain an undergraduate degree and then go to dental school for four years. In the UK, dentists can work either for

Figure 6.1 Applicants and Admissions in UK Dental Schools, 1980–2001

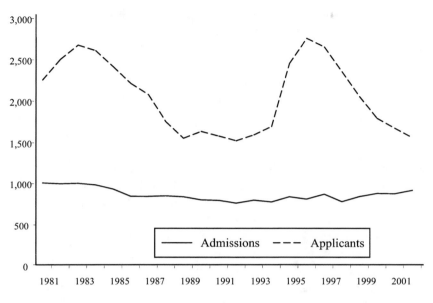

SOURCE: Jetha (2002).

the national health insurance or as a private dentist. Within the national health insurance, there are proscribed numbers of patients per day, and this often leaves little time per patient.

Unlike the United States, where dentists and their perceptions of labor market conditions often influence dental licensing boards, the numbers who enter the occupation in a particular year in the UK, and the number of overall entrants, are largely determined by the demands of the national health insurance through the national government acting as a planner (Kleiner 1990; Maurizi 1974). As shown in Figure 6.1, even though there are booms and busts in the number of applicants, perhaps following the "Cobweb model" of either too many or too few practitioners based on the previous year's market conditions, the number of admittances remained constant over time from 1980 to 2001 (Jetha 2002). It is unclear if the constant number of admittances to dental school is impacted more by the dental association or by general health policy through the national health insurance in Britain. To the extent that there were shortages, any increase in demand for dentists was dealt with largely through an increase in foreign dentists practicing in the UK (Jetha 2002).

For most of the medical fields in the EU, the process of entering a government-regulated occupation is similar. The port of entry, which is usually an educational establishment, determines the number of practitioners, with generally no state-sponsored exam following graduation from the national government-approved curriculum. In the United States, constraints on entry often are more difficult, as a consequence of longer years of schooling and entry tests following graduation. In the EU, however, licensing regulations are focused on the practice of the occupation. In a ranking of regulatory policies of EU professions in comparison with the United States, Garoupa (2004) finds that, based on criteria of "libertarian, efficiency, and consumer protection," the United States has the "best regulatory framework" for improving market performance. Other examinations of licensing for EU nations have been developing indices of regulation for a number of occupations to include accountants, architects, engineers, and pharmacists, in addition to physicians and lawyers (Paterson, Fink, and Ogus 2003). These factors include entry, fees, organizational forms, advertising, and conduct restrictions for doctors and lawyers. In the medical professions, more than 50 percent work for the government in the UK, whereas only 20 percent work for the government in the United States (Robinson and Dixon 1999). Moreover, for France and Germany, prices are largely established by the state-funded health care system, resulting in a reduction in hourly earnings (Busse and Riesberg 2004; Sandier, Paris, and Polton 2004). A ranking of EU countries by levels of licensing restrictions, using behavioral restrictiveness for doctors and lawyers, is shown in Figure 6.2. The figure shows that the United States has the lowest level of occupational restrictiveness relative to the EU nations on behavioral restrictions for these universally regulated occupations.

Recently, the EU has stated that their goal for regulated occupations is to examine price fixing, recommended prices, advertising regulations, entry requirements, reserved rights, and regulations governing business structure (Commission of the European Communities 2004). The general rule is that when a nation in the EU delegates "its policy-making power to a professional association without sufficient safeguards, that is without clearly indicating the public interest objectives to respect, without retaining the last word and without control of the implementation,

Figure 6.2 Measures of Post-Entry Restrictions for Doctors and Lawyers in the United States and the EU

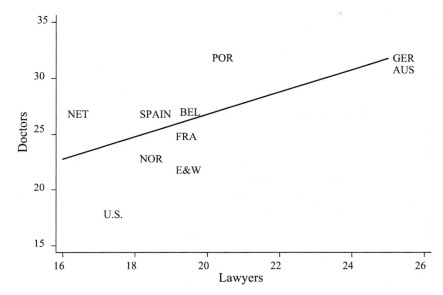

NOTE: Estimates modify the index in Garoupa (2004) to include only post-entry restriction on work, using only integer values, and having lower values indicates fewer restrictions. Nations evaluated include the United States, Netherlands, Spain, Norway, Belgium, France, England and Wales (E&W), Portugal, Germany, and Austria.

the Member State can also be held liable for any resulting infringement" (Commission of the European Communities 2004, p. 6). The focus of the EU rules is on attempting to ensure that the government and not the professional associations have the major voice in the regulation of the professions. Nevertheless, current policies on occupational regulation are generally much more restrictive than those in the United States following entry into the occupation.[2]

The professional occupations are of particular interest in the EU since this sector is growing at a much faster pace than overall employment, much like in the United States. From 1980 to 1990, employment in this more highly regulated category (in the OECD countries reporting data) grew by an average of 55 percent, six times faster than the overall national employment growth of 9 percent (Biggar and Wise 2000, p. 44). More recently, professional occupations in the EU during the first half of 2003 continued to outpace overall employment. Overall employment grew at an annual rate of 0.7 percent while employment in occupations that were regulated in the service sector grew by 5 percent (Commission of the European Communities 2004, p. 8). In part, as a consequence of this employment growth among more highly regulated occupations, the EU is monitoring licensing among member countries through its commission on competition.

As part of these reforms in the labor market, mobility for most occupations has grown (Jeffery 2001). In 2003, the EU made it easier for individuals in most occupations to move between nations without additional regulatory constraints by requiring mutual recognition of occupational requirements, similar to endorsement among states in the United States (Lonbay 2004). However, language and cultural factors are more likely to serve as barriers to geographic mobility in the EU relative to the United States (Krueger 2000). An occupation that is exempted from these reduced barriers is attorneys, who still maintain national requirements without "endorsement" across EU countries.

GOVERNMENTAL LIMITATIONS ON REGULATED OCCUPATIONS IN THE EU

Although mobility across nations has become easier within the EU, there still remain constraints on the behavioral aspects of working in the EU. Many of the countries in the EU maintain restrictions on advertising, fees, relationships with other businesses, foreign providers of services, and location of business or practice (Bertrand and Kramarz 2001). Unlike in the United States, where professions come under antitrust legislation as discussed in Chapter 2, the basic legislation on restrictive trade practices in the UK does not apply to professional services, but professional conduct may fall under the monopoly provisions of the legislation.

The Director General of Fair Trading (DGFT) in the UK considers that the principles of competition policy and law should be applied to the business and market activities of all professions as they apply to other business activities. There have been several transformations in UK laws governing occupational regulation that have reduced regulations.

Moreover, government policy is to increase competition, and some of the professions have themselves embarked on reforms designed to foster greater competition in their various business activities.

In France, the Conseil de la concurrence, the major regulatory agency, has stated that professional organization rules may not authorize violations of the rules of competition law, notably those against price-fixing agreements. The Conseil has condemned a boycott by local architects intended to maintain fee levels. And the Conseil has challenged three local bar associations' fee schedules, emphasizing that they had an anticompetitive effect even when they may not have been adopted for an anticompetitive purpose. The authority for this action was established by a 1987 decision involving fee schedules of architects, which was affirmed by the courts in 1992. A closely aligned issue is the regulations on opening new establishments in specific locations. In France, local merchants must approve the establishment of a new business, and the process is likely to eliminate competition in licensed occupations such as attorneys, accountants, and architects on a geographic or location-specific basis (Bertrand and Kramarz 2001). The estimates suggest that this regulatory practice reduces overall job growth by 10 percent.

In Germany, regulation of professions occurs both through the government and through industry associations. In part as a consequence of heavy regulation and resulting constraints of most occupations, there has been a movement toward deregulation. Germany still requires 41 professions, from well diggers to chimney sweeps, to pass exams to get a "Meisterbrief," or master certificate, before they start a business. Local organizations are required to hire these individuals or face governmental financial penalties or sanctions.

From 1995 to 2003, Germany has exempted 53 of 94 trades from having to pass qualifying exams, reducing the number of licensed workers in the Zentraverband Des Deutschen Handwerks (ZDH), which is the occupation/business federation, from 6.3 million in 1995 to 4.8 million in 2003. Generally, the movement toward deregulation has included lower-risk jobs such as hairdressers and florists. Nevertheless, German businesses, government, and unions see the rules as guarantees of the nation's traditional emphasis on quality products and services (Miller 2004).

ESTIMATES OF THE IMPACT OF LICENSING ON
EARNINGS, BY COUNTRY

There are substantial differences in the method by which licensing impacts workers and wages in the United States and Europe. In the United States, there are greater barriers to entry as a consequence of longer general and specific training periods and the requirement for the passage of a licensing exam. Moreover, for most professions, the cost of education is borne by the individual. In contrast, in most EU countries, subsidies for education are higher so that debt for entering an occupation is lower. However, there are greater constraints on behavioral issues like advertising and fees. Moreover, the lower levels of wage inequality in the EU relative to the United States may make the gains to licensing lower in the EU.

In this section I provide estimates of the impact of licensing on hourly earnings for three of the largest EU nations: the UK, France, and Germany. The methodology used is similar to that employed in analyzing licensing on earnings in the United States in Chapter 4. I first compare certain licensed occupations to their unlicensed counterparts in each nation and then provide an overall estimate of the impact on licensing in the EU. Unlike U.S. census data, which has large numbers of observations, the analysis of the EU nations is based on either administrative data or surveys that contain smaller sample sizes in large part due to either the difficulty of sharing this information with non-nationals or the lack of wage or earnings data from these sources because of concerns regarding confidentiality within their countries.

United Kingdom

The UK has been concerned with and has been working to change its competition law governing regulated occupations for more than 30 years (Siebert 1977). The policy has been to increase competition, and many of the professions have implemented programs in order to implement directives on the deregulation of the professions. More specifically, the Competition Act of 1998 replaced several more restrictive policies on regulated occupations. One important provision was the "complex monopoly" provision, under which several persons who are not connected but who together account for at least one-quarter of the supply or acquisition of any particular goods or services in all or part of the UK can be examined by the Competition Commission. They can be investigated if they are engaged in conduct that has or is likely to have the effect of restricting, distorting, or preventing competition. This provision dealt with issues of the structure of services and the linkages of accounting and law firms. One of the policies focusing on licensing was the freedom to advertise and to set prices competitively, which is now widely accepted in the regulated professions in the UK.

The analysis for the UK uses data from the Labour Force Survey, which is similar to the CPS in the United States. Given the sample size of the UK survey and the categorization of occupations within the survey, the occupations that are examined are somewhat different from those in the United States, since occupations with fewer members are excluded. The licensed occupations in the analysis include dentists, lawyers, pharmacists, physicians, and school teachers. The comparisons with unlicensed occupations are based on the same "occupation family" by the Dictionary of Occupational Titles in a manner similar to the comparisons developed in Chapter 4. The estimation methodology also is similar to that presented in Chapter 4, in which earnings of similar licensed and unlicensed occupations in the United States were examined. The counterfactual analysis builds on a "thought experiment" of what would have been the earnings outcome if all the measured human capital characteristics of one group were given to the other group, except for licensing. For example, using this approach assumes that the market rewards individuals differently for each year of schooling, age, or experience based on whether the individual was licensed. In order to do the statistical analysis of developing a counterfactual for this issue, a decomposition analysis is implemented. This procedure presumes little movement between occupational groups and that all differences between the two groups not accounted for by human capital and other factors are a consequence of licensing. For each person in the regulated occupation, the model predicts what would have been the earnings of the individual if they were not regulated at the mean of the distribution.[3] Given the smaller sample size of the observations in the British data, the comparison occupations were more limited than those for the United States estimates.

Table 6.2 Hourly Earnings in Selected Licensed and Unlicensed Occupations in the UK

Occupation	Actual difference	Difference due to	
		Nonlicensing factors	Licensing
Medical practitioners			
Chemists	0.16	0.04	0.12
Biological scientists and biochemists	0.21	−0.01	0.23
Pharmacists, pharmacologists			
Chemists	0.04	−0.02	0.06
Biological scientists and biochemists	0.10	−0.10	0.20
Dental practitioners			
Chemists	0.35	0.00	0.35
Biological scientists and biochemists	0.40	−0.10	0.50
Secondary education teachers			
Administrators— national government	0.07	0.12	−0.05
Lawyers and judges			
University, polytechnic teachers	0.02	−0.14	0.17

SOURCE: UK Labour Force Survey, 1993–1997, $N = 13,562$.

Table 6.2 gives the estimates of the impact of being in a licensed occupation relative to an unregulated occupation in the UK using data from the British Labour Force Survey for medical practitioners, pharmacists, dental practitioners, teachers, and lawyers. These occupations were selected in large part due to data availability within the Labour Force Survey. Based on the results in Table 6.2, the UK has relatively open markets for licensed occupations, with advertising allowed for most professions. The estimates show that, when human capital variables are accounted for, licensing factors show much variation on earnings, from zero for secondary teachers to as much as 35 to 50 percent for dentists. In comparison to the U.S. estimates, the impact of licensing in the UK has similar relative effects, but the absolute percent impacts are smaller. For example, the average licensing impact in the United States for physicians and dentists relative to their peer occupations as shown in Table 4.4 is 41 and 64 percent, but it is between 12 and 50 percent in the UK for these two occupations. For the other occupations in Table 6.2, such as lawyers and pharmacists, the licensing premium is between 6 and 20 percent. The only occupation for which licensing has no real impact in the table is teachers, and this result is similar to the impact in the United States. It may be that since teachers work mainly for the public or for a large educational organization in the UK, there is a small negative impact on earnings due to the ability of employers to argue and lobby for a large supply of practitioners that may dominate any impact of licensing. Overall, for the regulated occupations in the UK, there are more constraints than in the United States, but these results suggest that the outcomes result in licensing having smaller but still substantial impacts on earnings relative to their comparison group.

France

Figure 6.2, which compares post-entry restrictions among EU nations, shows that, at least for doctors and lawyers, France has a more restrictive system of regulation than either the United States or the UK, but it is less restrictive than Germany. A more recent categorization of regulation for EU nations for accountants, architects, and pharmacists gives evidence that France is substantially more regulated for these occupations than the UK but slightly less so than in Germany (Paterson, Fink, and Ogus 2003). Entry requirements and the way that business can be conducted are the common methods of developing these indices. The criteria for measuring restrictions are through fixed prices, regulation of advertising and marketing, the regulation of location and diversification on offering services, and restrictions on interprofessional cooperation (e.g., restrictions on forms of business). This pattern of relative restrictiveness for France is also likely to apply to other regulated occupations in the nation.

Table 6.3 gives evidence on the impact of licensing relative to their comparison occupations in France for the years 1990 to 1997 using the Enquêtes Emploi. Given the limited sample size of this database, the analysis only allows an examination of a few regulated occupations,

Table 6.3   Hourly Earnings in Selected Licensed and Unlicensed Occupations in France, 1990–1997

Occupation	Actual difference	Difference due to	
		Nonlicensing factors	Licensing
Doctor			
Higher education teachers	−0.05	−0.23	0.18
Programmers	0.35	0.28	0.08
Dentist			
Higher education teachers	−0.02	−0.21	0.19
Programmers	0.37	0.28	0.10
Teacher			
Social workers	−0.01	0.00	−0.01

NOTE: $N = 15{,}579$.
SOURCE: "Enquêtes Emploi," National Institute for Statistics and Economic Studies (INSEE) (1998).

including doctors, dentists, and teachers. The technique in examining licensing is similar to that employed for the UK and the United States. For each person in the regulated occupation, the model predicts what would have been the earnings of the individual if they were not regulated at the mean of the distribution. The results show that dentists and doctors earn more relative to their comparison groups using this data. For both doctors and dentists, the estimated impact of licensing is between 8 and 19 percent relative to its comparison occupations, which is below the comparable estimates in both the UK and the United States. Greater regulation in the way business is conducted in France likely results in these licensed occupations having lower relative earnings. Furthermore, most workers in medical occupations work for the government or receive payments from the government in France, and this is likely to limit wage growth. The estimates for teachers use a registered occupation, social workers, rather than a licensed occupation as a comparison group. In France, social workers fit under the category of being in a registered occupation noted, as "the inappropriate use of the title of social worker by unqualified individuals" is illegal (International Federation of Social Workers 2004, p. 21). Nevertheless, they are allowed to do the work as long as they do not call themselves social workers.

Consequently, teachers, who are licensed, are compared to a "registered occupation." The estimates in Table 6.3 show there is no earnings premium for teachers relative to social workers. Overall, there appears to be a licensing wage premium for these licensed occupations, but the impact is smaller than for either the United States or the UK.

Germany

Using the indices of EU occupational licensing, Germany, along with Austria, is usually ranked among the most regulated nations in the EU (Garoupa 2004; Paterson, Fink, and Ogus 2003). This result is mainly a consequence of regulations on practice following entry into the occupation. As Figure 6.2 shows, regulations on post-entry market restrictions on working are among the highest in Germany relative to the other EU nations. Similarly, for other licensed occupations such as accountants, architects, engineers, and pharmacists, Germany has the highest values in these post-entry restrictiveness indices. More recently, Germany has been moving toward deregulating its labor markets as evidenced by the reduction in the number of occupations licensed and the move toward the adoption of OECD policies on the regulation of the professions (Biggar and Wise 2000).

Unfortunately, the data used for examining regulations for Germany contain the fewest number of observations relative to the data available for the United States, UK, and France. The data from the Qualifikation

Table 6.4 Hourly Earnings in Selected Licensed and Unlicensed Occupations in Germany, 1991

Occupation	Actual difference	Difference due to	
		Nonlicensing factors	Licensing
Dentist			
Computer scientist	−0.05	−0.06	0.01
Chemist	−0.09	−0.13	0.05
Doctor			
Chemist	−0.08	−0.09	0.01

NOTE: $N = 1{,}493$.
SOURCE: "Qualifikation und Berufsverlauf."

und Berufsverlauf contain only 1,493 observations for the year 1991. Nevertheless, in Table 6.4, the approach for the analysis examines each person in the regulated occupation, and the model predicts what would have been the earnings of the individual if the occupation were not regulated. Given the small sample size, the analysis focuses only on doctors and dentists and also has a limited number of comparison occupations that are in the same job family. The results show that dentists only made between 1 and 5 percent more than the designated control group as a consequence of licensing. The licensing premium for doctors relative to chemists is less than 1 percent. These estimates suggest that Germany, with its higher level of regulation, especially following entry into an occupation, has a lower licensing premium for dentists and doctors than the other two countries in the EU analysis. The lower impact of licensing on earnings is consistent with results of small returns to education effects in Germany. Pischke and vonWachter (2005) speculate that the reason for low returns to education may be a result of rigid wages in Germany, the existence of the apprenticeship training system, or the better academic skills provided earlier in the German system. Nevertheless, the returns to licensing in these occupations are also much lower in Germany than in the other nations examined in this chapter.

IMPACT OF LICENSING ON EARNINGS IN THE UK, FRANCE, AND GERMANY

The UK, France, and Germany comprised about 51 percent of the EU workforce prior to the expansion of the EU in 2003 and represent a relatively lightly regulated (UK), a medium-regulated (France), and a highly regulated (Germany) nation with respect to the rigor with which they regulate occupations. However, to what extent does licensing impact the earnings of a group of regulated and similar unregulated individuals in these occupations? Table 6.5 shows the impact of licensing on hourly earnings in these three countries with standard human capital control variables such as age, age-squared, gender, years of education, and whether the person had a college degree. The occupations examined are presented in the note to the table, and the estimates show a somewhat smaller variety of occupations than those presented for the

Table 6.5 Impact of Licensing on Hourly Earnings in the UK, France, and Germany

	Coefficient	Standard error
Licensed occupation	0.011*	0.006
Age	0.063*	0.002
Age^2	−0.001	0.000
Female	−0.094*	0.005
Education (year)	0.039*	0.001
University education	0.394*	0.032
Constant	1.55	0.05
R^2	0.79	
N	28,326	

NOTE: With dummy variable controls for country: UK and France relative to Germany and year of the observation. The coefficients for the country dummy variables are interpreted in comparison to the base country, Germany. *Indicates statistical significance at the 0.05 level. Occupations in the sample include doctors, dentists, accountants, public administrators, higher education teachers, engineers (chemistry), teachers, social workers, programmers, administrators—national government, personnel training managers, chemists, biological scientists and biochemists, medical practitioners (nondoctors), pharmacists, pharmacologists, dental practitioners (not dentists), university and polytechnic teachers, etc., secondary education teachers, etc., primary and nursery education teachers, lawyers and judges, chartered and certified accountants, actuaries, economists, and statisticians.

United States in Chapter 4. This set of occupations is smaller because the sources of data for EU nations do not have a sufficiently large number of persons in the occupations for a more expansive analysis. The estimates show that licensing has a modest but statistically significant 1 percent impact on hourly earnings. The estimate is much smaller than the 10 to 12 percent impact in the United States and may be a consequence of greater post-entry restrictions on competition that limit prices and earnings relative to those occupations that can advertise, charge market fees, and establish contingency fees based on outcomes. Moreover, the generally higher taxes and social benefits in the EU reduce overall income inequality in the EU, and this also is the case for regulated occupations that have only a slight earnings edge relative to their unlicensed counterparts. In addition, a much higher percentage of the individuals work for the government or have government-determined fees in these occupations in the EU and consequently have narrower variance in their range of income. To the extent that there are little to no measurable quality benefits, the potential "dead-weight losses" in the EU are lower than in the United States. However, economic losses could be substantial if the reduction in job growth is similar to the 10 percent estimate that Bertrand and Kramarz (2001) found as a consequence of regulatory restrictions of businesses. These estimates of dead-weight loss could be even higher if the economic value of "wait time" for a doctor or other health service professional were included in a calculation. Since there is no comprehensive value on the number or the percentage of the workforce that is licensed in the EU, these types of calculations are difficult. Moreover, there has not been the large body of research into the quality effects of occupational licensing in the EU relative to the studies completed in the United States, so that an overall assessment of the impact of licensing for these three nations is difficult to estimate.

IMPLICATIONS FOR OCCUPATIONAL REGULATION

This examination of licensing in Europe provides a useful comparison relative to the United States. The focus of U.S. licensing is on control of entry and mobility across states, with little attention to the prices charged, method of payment, or the barriers to advertising. In contrast, it is somewhat easier and usually takes a shorter time for entry into the professions in the EU. For most occupations, entering the education process occurs immediately after high school, though being accepted is highly competitive. Students matriculate into the professions and usually finish their professional education, which is subsidized in large part by the government, at an earlier age than in the United States. Following entry, there tend to be many more constraints on work, including location, prices charged, and the lack of opportunity to provide information to consumers on the quality of the service through advertising. In the licensed health professions, the employer is often the government. Consequently, it is not surprising to find that earnings of professionals relative to their comparison group are lower in the UK, France, and Germany than they are in the United States.

Unfortunately, there have been no analytical examinations of the impact that licensing in these nations has on the quality of service received in the EU. This stands in contrast to the large number of studies that have examined licensing in the United States. For the most part, the empirical work shows that licensing has modest to no impact on quality relative to a regime of certification or registration. Moreover, there is little evidence that insurance companies in the United States give discounts for malpractice insurance to individuals who are licensed relative to their unlicensed counterparts.

In summary, the impact of licensing within the three countries examined in this chapter shows that regulation has a modest 1 percent impact on the earnings of the regulated occupations. This stands in stark contrast to the 10 to 12 percent impact for regulated to unregulated occupations or the 4 percent effect for those occupations licensed in some states and not in others in the United States. The impact of licensing must therefore be viewed in the context of the nation that is regulating the workers. If national inequality is low and constraints on the occupation are high, then price and wage impacts are likely to be modest. On the other hand, the impact of this regulatory policy where there are few financial incentives to succeed may lead to less effort because wage variations are small or the more able seek occupations where the financial constraints are less limited. In addition, innovation, creativity, and employment may be reduced in the regulated sector, as relative financial incentives for more effort in the regulated sector are small, but entry requirements are tough.

Notes

1. The state of Wisconsin is unique in that it has a provision that allows graduating law students in the two major law schools in the state (i.e., the University of Wisconsin and Marquette University) to not be required to take the state licensing exam if they agree to practice in the state for at least five years (Wisconsin Court System 2005). This policy is similar to the procedures to become licensed for this occupation in most EU countries.
2. This lower level of post-entry regulation largely occurred following the *Goldfarb v. Virginia* (1975) decision (discussed in Chapter 2) and its enforcement in a vigorous way by the FTC and the Antitrust Division of the Department of Justice.
3. Given the small number of observations by country in these data, no nonparametric estimates were developed like those for the United States in Chapter 4.

7

The Emerging Labor Market Institution of Occupational Licensing

> *Not long ago the Governor of a Midwestern state was approached by a representative of a particular trade anxious to enlist the Governor's support in securing passage of legislation to license their trade.*
>
> *"Governor," the man said, "passage of this licensing act will ensure that only qualified people will practice this occupation; it will eliminate charlatans, incompetents or frauds; and it will thereby protect the safety of the people of this state."*
>
> *The Governor, from long experience, was somewhat skeptical. "Gentlemen," he asked, "are you concerned with advancing the health, safety and welfare of the people under the police powers of this state or are you primarily interested in creating a monopoly situation and eliminate competition and raise prices?"*
>
> *The spokesman for the occupational group smiled and said, "Governor, we're interested in a little of each."*
>
> —Council of State Governments (1952, p.1)

As the above exchange illustrates, the potential conflict between enhancing quality and restricting competition has been at the core of the debate on the efficacy of occupational licensing during the post–World War II era. The goal of this concluding chapter is to provide a further rationale for the existence, impact, and potential policy implications of occupational licensing. This concluding analysis examines the issue of the benefits and costs of standardization, which licensing encourages through regulatory boards. I provide new evidence on how employment growth differs according to whether or not occupations are regulated by a state. I then summarize the other major empirical and theoretical contributions of the book. To conclude, I present policy implications of the analysis presented in this book, with an emphasis on different forms of regulation that may provide most of the benefits of licensing but without many of the increased costs of this form of regulation.

The development of the regulation of occupations and trades has a long and varied history. Workers who do the same tasks have gotten together both to improve the quality of work and to restrict the number of workers who are available to work at the job since early civilization (Gross 1984). As Chapter 2 details, the development in Europe of the history of trades and guilds had the effect of limiting social mobility and restricting competition, yet it provided economic and social benefits of greater human capital investment (Scoville 1969). In the United States in the latter part of the nineteenth century, associations representing occupations were successful in getting the mechanism of the state both to establish minimum levels of education and other characteristics necessary for entry into occupations and to limit entry into the occupation. Although there is evidence to suggest that these policies were able to increase some measures of quality in the periods immediately following enactment of the laws, the long-term impact of these licensing laws was to give the occupations a monopoly on the tasks in the occupation (Law and Kim 2004). Occupational regulation has evolved largely as a state or local issue rather than a national policy, unlike the national preemption of most other labor laws.

As the opening quote of this chapter implies, there is often an implicit political economy trade-off occurring in the regulation of occupations. A precondition for licensing is the existence of a group of workers with a basic skill level, a commonality of tasks, work that has a level of substitutability with others, and a density of population that is organized in the political jurisdiction. The workers want higher wages and, because they are in skilled jobs, the consequences of those jobs being performed badly can be negative for the consumer or the community. The social deal that is struck between the workers and society is that there is some quality guarantee in return for restrictions on who can do the work, that is, weeding out the "charlatans, incompetents or frauds." The restrictions on entry continue over time and, especially once the licensed occupation has coalesced, any pressure for substantial future increases in quality may be much weaker, but the restrictions on entry generate work and pay benefits.

EMERGENCE OF OCCUPATIONAL LICENSING

In contrast to the decline of labor market institutions and regulations, such as unions and the federal minimum wages during the latter
half of the twentieth century and beginning of the twenty-first century,
occupational licensing has seen a steady growth of coverage to at least
one-fifth of the U.S. workforce. In contrast to unions, whose members
work in industries that are declining while facing strong employer opposition, licensed occupations exist mainly in the service industries,
which are growing much more rapidly than the overall economy and
more rapidly than other industries, such as manufacturing (Eckstein
and Nagypal 2004; Kleiner 2002). Occupation associations face little
employer opposition in forming associations at work. Often employee
associations are welcome within an organization because they bring
about a sense of professionalism or emphasis on quality that may enhance workplace productivity. In some cases they serve as a "works
council" for the members of the occupation, often discussing with management both how conditions could be improved at work and how the
employees in the occupation can contribute to the economic success of
the organization. By having an organized occupation group within an
organization, employers can gain information about the enterprise from
employees without the wage premium that unions exact at the establishment level (Freeman and Lazear 1995).

Through the use of licensing at the local, state, or national level,
employers' decisions about hiring regulated employees are taken out
of competition from unregulated groups who cannot do the work by
the actions of the government. Consequently, employers who hire, for
example, teachers, doctors, nurses, librarians, and electricians must
only employ individuals with certain credentials to do certain tasks.
This results in the elimination of other options or substitutes in the labor market. Licensed occupations have been able to achieve what very
few unions (except those that are allowed to have "closed-shop" labor
agreements) have been able to accomplish by restricting labor supply.[1]
Employers are required to hire only persons who are members of the
licensed group. Consequently, it is not surprising that there are a licensing employment impact and a wage premium.

THE BENEFITS AND COSTS OF STANDARDIZATION

One of the potential benefits of regulation is to establish a common body of knowledge or skills within the occupation as well as provide consumers with a more homogenous service than would exist without regulation. Education levels, testing, and other forms of background checks provide this standardization of the job-related quality of human resources supplied to the occupation. More recently state boards, in co-operation with occupational associations, have proscribed standard procedures that are appropriate for the occupation, such as those for dentists and dental hygienists. This process further standardizes the type of service that is given to consumers. A major argument for the licensing of occupations is that it eliminates the downside risk of seeking services from an occupation. If testing and background checks "eliminate charlatans, incompetents or frauds," as the opening lines of this chapter imply, then consumers may be willing to pay a higher price for the service offered by occupational licensing.

A review of the body of research from experimental economics and psychology shows that consumers value the reduction in downside risk more than they value the potential benefits of a positive outcome (Kahneman, Knetsch, and Thaler 1991). The preference by consumers of the status quo or reducing risk of a highly negative outcome has been called "loss aversion," which is an element of "prospect theory" developed by Kahneman and Tversky (1979). For example, the utility to society may be greater by minimizing the likelihood of a poor diagnosis as a consequence of going to a poor doctor because the incompetents have been weeded out as a result of licensing. Consequently, the perceived benefits of a nonstandard but potentially highly positive outcome of going to an unlicensed biomedical research scientist still may not be worth it. Using the power of the state to both limit the downside risk of poor quality care and reduce the possibility of an upside benefit may be a trade-off that maximizes consumer utility or welfare. Evidence of the acceptance of this trade-off is the growth of licensing of occupations across virtually all states during the past century. Consistent with the experimental economics research on financial theory, the risk of a loss has much greater utility than the possibility of a large gain (Kahneman, Knetsch, and Thaler 1991). The results in this literature show that the selling price of a product that is the "possession" of an individual is much greater than the auction price or the price for which a like possession could be purchased in the market as a replacement. The avoidance of loss may be a major reason for the persuasive arguments for licensing.

The gains from an unregulated service might include potential benefits from free market competition, such as lower prices and greater innovation, without the constraints of a regulatory body such as a licensing board. This upside potential gain can be through the use of nonstandard methods or new research that has not yet been approved by the licensing agency as appropriate for the service (Rottenberg 1980). Deviations from prescribed methods of providing a service are discouraged by licensing boards and may even be found to be illegal by a state board. For example, not having a dentist on site is illegal when providing a service such as teeth cleaning. Dental hygienists are not allowed to "practice" without a dentist on site, with the "site" being defined by statute or the dental board. Although this policy protects against downside losses of finding a major problem that may require immediate attention, it reduces the ability of the hygienist to provide only the service that is most useful to the patient. Moreover, there is little leeway for the dental service industry to provide new or innovative services without being found in violation of the state licensing laws. It may in some cases be an example of the labor relations concept of "featherbedding," in which dentists are on the premises but do little work.

Voters, through the political process, often prefer to reduce the downside of any service. The outcome of "risk aversion" comes at the expense of having the upside of any service reduced. This preference provides consumers the benefit of perceived higher quality through higher levels of regulation (Leland 1979). However, from the evidence I was able to gather, there is no overall quality benefit (measured in a number of different ways) of licensing to consumers. Consequently, the cost of regulation to society is higher prices or longer waits for a service. An additional societal cost is the reallocation of income from consumers to practitioners of the licensed occupation as well as lost output. The cost of licensing is an element that consumers should take into account as part of their evaluation of this labor market institution relative to other forms of regulation.

EMPLOYMENT GROWTH OF THE SAME OCCUPATIONS IN
REGULATED AND UNREGULATED STATES

Chapter 1 noted the overall change in employment of licensed occupations relative to the workforce in the United States. Overall, the
values were similar, but with the more rapid growth of service employment during the 1990s, where most individuals in licensed occupations
are employed, the expectation was that employment growth would have
been much higher in the regulated occupations relative to overall employment. Based on the theory and evidence in the economics of regulation, occupational licensing can reduce employment in the occupation
within a political jurisdiction such as a state or city. However, by reducing "lemons" in the market, regulation can also increase the demand for
the service and thereby increase employment. A more straightforward
way to analyze which impact is greater is to focus on occupations that
are licensed in some states and not in others. This analysis would allow an examination of the ability of the regulated states to maintain
employment restrictions and the effect of the increased perceptions of
quality on employment in comparison to the unregulated states. Three
occupations in the censuses for 1990 and 2000 meet the criteria of being
regulated in approximately the same number of states and having about
the same number of workers in regulated and unregulated states: librarians, respiratory therapists, and dietitians and nutritionists.

Table 7.1 gives estimates of the employment growth for librarians,
respiratory therapists, and dietitians and nutritionists from 1990 to 2000
in those states that regulate these occupations relative to those who do
not. In 2000, librarians were licensed in 19 states, respiratory therapists in 35 states, and dietitians and nutritionists in 36 states. The results in the table show that for occupations that experienced declines in
employment during the decade, such as librarians and dietitians, those
states that license the occupations saw employment for practitioners
decline at an even faster rate than those that did not regulate them. For
example, librarian overall employment declined by approximately 7
percent over the decade of the 1990s, but this decline was composed of
a 5.3 percent decline in the unregulated sector and a 9.2 percent decline
in the regulated sector. Similarly, the overall decline in employment
for dietitians and nutritionists over the decade was 9.5 percent, but the

Table 7.1 Comparing Employment Growth of Occupations in Regulated and Unregulated States

	Librarians		Respiratory therapists		Dietitians and nutritionists	
	1990	2000	1990	2000	1990	2000
Number in occupation	215,680	200,060	63,560	86,956	94,360	85,480
% licensed in occupation	50.2	49.2	49.8	49.5	49.5	47.2
Change in employment (%)						
Unlicensed states		−5.3		37.6		−5.2
Licensed states		−9.2		35.9		−13.7

SOURCE: 1990 and 2000 censuses, regulatory status in 2000.

decline was 5.2 percent in the unlicensed states and 13.7 percent in the licensed states. However, for respiratory therapists, an occupation that experienced rapid growth in employment, the differences in the growth rates between regulated and unregulated states was only 1.7 percentage points.

In order to provide additional statistical rigor to the analysis, I estimated a difference-in-difference regression analysis of the impact of licensing on the employment change within occupations that have an approximately even division between licensed and unlicensed practitioners based on the estimates in Table 7.1. The approach combines the three partially regulated occupations (librarians, respiratory therapists, and dietitians and nutritionists) from 1990 to 2000 and compares the percent employment change with both fully licensed occupations (lawyers, dentists, and cosmetologists) and unlicensed occupations (economists, computer programmers, and glaziers). These occupations were selected based on availability of data in the 1990 and 2000 censuses and the inclusion of high and relatively lower levels of educational attainment. The results are presented in Table 7.2. The difference-in-difference approach gives regression estimates and compares the percent employment growth due to licensing occupations in some states and not others with the growth rates of both fully licensed occupations and unlicensed ones for each state. The overall impact across all the occupations in the sample of regulated, unregulated, and partially regulated occupations shows that licensing reduces the percentage growth rate by a statistically significant 20 percent over the 1990 to 2000 period. One interpretation of this result is that an occupation that was licensed and grew at a 10 percent rate from 1990 to 2000 would have grown at a 12 percent rate without regulation. These estimates indicate that this form of regulation serves as a barrier to employment growth within an occupation rather than enhancing the perceived quality that generates more demand for the services within the occupation, which may in turn lead to gains in wages, as shown in Chapter 4.

The basic means presented in Table 7.1 show that, for those occupations where there is a decline in the demand for their services and employment is in decline, licensing barriers may serve to further discourage new entrants into the occupation. The commonly viewed barriers to entry (e.g., additional years of schooling, licensing exams, and residency requirements) can serve to further discourage individuals

Table 7.2 Difference-in-Difference Estimate of the Impact of Licensing on Percent Employment Change for Partially Licensed Occupations, 1990–2000

Licensed state (percentage growth rate)	−0.20
	(0.07)
State controls	Yes
All nine occupation controls	Yes
R^2	0.34
Number of state level observations	450

NOTE: Partially licensed occupations included are librarians, respiratory therapists, and dietitians and nutritionists. Controls included percent employment changes for universally licensed occupations: lawyers, dentists, and cosmetologists, and unlicensed occupations: economists, sociologists, and glaziers. Standard error is in parentheses.

from choosing to enter an occupation in a state. Conversely, when an occupation is growing and there are higher expected returns in the form of higher pay and job security, then the licensing barriers appear to be a lesser constraint. For persons who are considering entering an occupation, these licensing barriers may be perceived as a fixed cost to be overcome by meeting the initial barriers. As occupations are growing, trade schools and universities also expand their educational programs to accommodate the growing demand for individuals in the occupation, and they are likely willing participants in the drive to regulate occupations as long as there are formal education requirements. Nevertheless, licensing seems to dampen employment growth as well as accelerate decline in employment in regulated states.

MAJOR FINDINGS

In this book, I have identified how occupational regulation impacts both the quality provided to consumers and the major labor market effects of this institution. Licensing usually emerges from occupational associations, like the American Bar Association, when they have the political clout and the organizational skills to lobby a state legislature and present a strong enough case for regulation. In general, this has been the trend for occupations seeking to become regulated. Occupational licensing started to expand in the United States during the 1880s and then accelerated during the twentieth century. Following World War II, there was strong growth in the number of occupations that became licensed, but that growth has diminished as legislatures are requiring new occupations to present stronger cases on how licensing versus certification or registration of the occupation can protect the public from poor or substandard services. Legislatures are also requiring justification of the potential impact of regulation on the number of practitioners. Nevertheless, the occupations that have recently become regulated, such as crane operators in Minnesota, are not necessarily ones that will benefit the public through greater public safety.

Table 7.3 provides the key findings of this book in a summary format. A key theoretical issue is that licensing can initially provide benefits to a profession and consumers through standardization of the service by increasing the likelihood that the individuals delivering the service meet certain standards. Consequently, through their elected representatives, consumers have determined that licensing provides the highest standard to ensure that "charlatans, incompetents or frauds" will not be allowed to provide the service. The result is that other lower-quality and lower-priced services are precluded from the market.

A key numerical value provided in this book is the basic estimate of the percentage of the workforce that is covered by licensing laws. About 20 percent of the workforce is covered by licensing laws in the United States. However, this value understates the actual value because the estimate only includes occupations listed by the Department of Labor and the U.S. Census Bureau. Many states have their own occupational titles that were not included in the general listing. Further, it fails to include city and county licenses, which impact workers in the construction trades and the public safety and health fields. Nevertheless, these estimates do give a consistent measure of licensing when comparing licensing coverage across states and over time.

Using generally available sources on complaints to regulatory boards, malpractice insurance rates, and other direct quality measures, I find that there is no clear impact of licensing on overall quality, although there is some evidence that tougher licensing requirements may benefit individuals who have lower point-of-sale prices through insurance or greater access to the service. In contrast, there appears to be a positive impact for those persons working in a regulated occupation.

Table 7.3 Major Findings of the Impact of Occupational Licensing on the Enhancement of Quality and the Restriction of Competition

Issue	Key findings
Estimate of percent of workforce covered by licensing	Department of Labor and U.S. Census Bureau data indicate the percent of workforce covered by licensing is approximately 20 percent, a growth of 11 percent over the past 15 years.
Hypothesized benefits of licensing	Increased standardization of services and reduction in the perceived "loss aversion" by consumers due to poor quality service.
Evidence of the benefits of licensing	Some evidence that the insured and higher-income individuals gain from stricter licensing, but no measurable impact on overall quality.
Price and wage effects of licensing	Licensing drives up prices, and the overall wage effect relative to unlicensed occupations in cross-section data is 10 to 12 percent, but impacts differ widely based on methods, occupations, and toughness of restrictions.
Licensing and employment growth	Within an occupation, the employment growth rate is approximately 20 percent higher in states that do not require licensing, but impacts differ widely based on the methods and occupations.
State variations in licensing	Much variation in the number of occupations licensed by states and the percent of the workforce covered by licensing laws. Case studies show political spending by the occupational associations to be an important factor for who gets regulated.
Redistribution and lost output due to licensing	Estimated redistribution effects to regulated occupations of between $116 billion and $139 billion in 2000 dollars and lost output of $34.8 billion and $41.7 billion per year, which is less than 0.1 percent of total consumption expenditures.
U.S. and EU comparisons	Both the economies regulate entry, but there is often no exam beyond university or trade school to obtain a license for many of the professions in the EU. EU nations regulate prices charged and the organizational structure of the professions to a greater extent than in the United States. Wage effects for licensing are around 1 percent using cross-section estimates, but the impacts vary widely based on methods, occupations, and toughness of restrictions.

For example, switching to a licensed occupation from an unregulated one raises wages by 17 percentage points in comparison to switching to an unregulated occupation from a regulated one. Working in a regulated occupation raises hourly wages to about 10 to 12 percent relative to similar unregulated occupations. This value is at the lower end of the range of the union wage premium in the United States. Working in the same occupation, but in a state that does not require licensing, raises hourly wages by 4 percent relative to an unregulated state. However, working in a state with tougher licensing requirements than other states within the same occupation appears to offer no statistically significant wage premium for the occupations that were examined. Since there was no finding of overall benefits, but there were increased costs of licensing, the impact of licensing on the redistribution of earnings toward regulated occupations is approximately $116 billion and $139 billion in 2000 dollars, and lost output is between $34.8 billion and $41.7 billion per year. However, this is less than 0.1 percent of total consumption expenditures annually. This may help explain why occupations are successful in lobbying for regulation but see little public opposition.

Table 7.3 also provides summary findings of the impact of licensing in the UK, France, and Germany with comparisons to the United States. The results show that licensing has a smaller impact in the EU than in the United States. A comparison of licensed occupations with similar unlicensed ones shows that the greater the regulation of the occupations in the three EU countries, the lower the wage gap between regulated and unregulated purveyors of the service. Using a large number of occupations for the analysis in the EU, I find that there is a 1 percent wage gap between licensed and unlicensed occupations. In Europe, unlike the United States, there are many more constraints on prices charged as well as in the organizational structure of licensed occupations. In the UK this results in complaints over the wait time to get medical attention, whereas the complaints in the United States are over the prices of health care services. However, nations such as Germany are deregulating many of their previously licensed occupations, suggesting that the regulation of occupations can be reversed (Miller 2004).

PUBLIC POLICY IMPLICATIONS

Globalization and Licensing

One of the immediate implications of different licensing laws in the United States and Europe is the impact of the globalization of labor markets. Trade agreements like the North American Free Trade Agreement (NAFTA) and the international General Agreement on Trade in Services (GATS) often have labor side agreements which call for the free mobility of labor across boundaries. Since most licensing laws in the United States are focused at the state level, international agreements can be voided or at least contested through state licensing laws. On the other side of the Atlantic, the nations in the EU have national laws that provide legal mobility across countries for most occupations, except attorneys. With EU expansion, member states have instituted temporary regulations to address mobility for regulated occupations to and from the 10 additional member states (Cyprus, the Czech Republic, Estonia, Hungary, Latvia, Lithuania, Malta, Poland, Slovakia, and Slovenia) that joined the EU on May 1, 2004. Given the generally lower mobility in the EU, as well as the language barriers to moving across countries, having relaxed licensing standards across countries is not the same threat to reduced competition among regulated services that it is in the United States. As barriers to trade and financial exchanges are reduced through regional and international trade agreements, it is not surprising to also have stated policies that focus on reducing barriers to services among more-developed nations. If this is the case, then the United States will need to modify its state-focused licensing regime to provide greater consistency with the national policies for the regulation of service providers in other Organisation for Economic Co-operation and Development (OECD) nations as well as for less-developed nations.

One example of an occupation that has much at stake in international agreements is accounting, which has been a lead occupation in the GATS negotiations to reduce barriers to trade in professional services (White 1999). Many argue that the only real benefit to being a Certified Public Accountant (CPA) is that the charter allows a CPA to sign an audit opinion. Nevertheless, as large business enterprises generally have become more international, their need for more international accounting services has grown. Despite the considerable international presence of the major accounting firms, virtually all countries maintain various types of restrictions that impede the flow of accounting services across borders. The consequences have been higher costs, poorer service to clients, and reduced efficiency, as well as lower-quality accounting and auditing standards in many countries (White 1999).

Policy Alternatives to Occupational Licensing

A common refrain heard from the public upon the discussion of policy alternatives to licensing is, "I would never go to an unlicensed . . . " Licensing has evolved as the preferred option to deal with issues of the quality of service rendered by individuals in the occupations. From the public's perspective, this means having the toughest form of regulation to protect against individuals who are potentially incompetent to perform specific tasks. If consumers have a high level of "loss aversion" relative to potential gains, then having a policy such as licensing may be optimal to avoid negative outcomes. On the other hand, weaker forms of regulation may provide consumers with many of the benefits of licensing, such as confidence that the provider of the service has met minimal levels of education and skill to perform the task, but with fewer of the restrictions on competition associated with licensing.

One such policy option is certification. It is now the second largest form of regulation in the United States, with more than 200 occupations being certified by at least one state agency (Brinegar and Schmitt 1992; Smith-Peters and Smith-Peters 1994). As detailed in Chapter 2, certification grants title (occupational right-to-title) protection to persons meeting predetermined standards. Those without certification may perform the duties of the occupation but may not use the title. This process maintains the incentives for individuals to invest in human capital but allows substitutes if consumers of the service perceive the prices rising relative to what consumers want. Another even less restrictive form of regulation is registration, which usually requires individuals to file their names, addresses, and qualifications with a government agency before practicing in the occupation. This form of regulation may include posting a bond or filing a fee with a state agency. Also, for occupations with clear employer oversight and control, such as loan officers, many occupations could move from being regulated to being unregulated.

One of the benefits of certification is that it allows consumers to choose whether to go to a practitioner who has the appropriate qualifications to call themselves a practitioner in a particular field. In addition, it provides a monitor, the government, to police the individuals in the occupation who may not have the appropriate credentials to call themselves "certified." Unlike licensing, work can be performed by individuals who do not meet all the requirements of certification, and uncertified individuals may work in the industry without penalty from the state. This gives consumers greater choice, and if the limited case study evidence from Minnesota and Wisconsin can be generalized, this form of regulation provides similar quality benefits but may help to keep prices of services lower than with the tighter barriers to entry and mobility imposed by licensing. For those purveyors of a service who receive repeat business, and where information is shared with potential customers, licensing, certification, or registration may be unnecessary because the information about the service is widely available. Consequently, these occupations are regulated by market forces.

To what extent does either certification or registration provide the protection against "loss aversion" that many consumers and politicians say licensing gives and which may be worth the costs of granting monopoly power to an occupation? In other words, consumers respond more to knowledge about bad services than good conditions, which suggests that they respond more to information that reduces their utility than to information that increases it and is consistent with prospect theory (Kahneman and Tversky 1979). To illustrate, for an uninformed consumer that is considering brain surgery, licensing provides the guarantee that the provider of a service has at least finished medical school and taken a licensing exam. Nevertheless, a doctor who specializes in pediatrics, and had never performed major surgery, could legally perform brain surgery under most state licensing laws. Under certification, anyone who is not a certified brain surgeon could not argue that they have completed the course and passed the appropriate exams and claim to be the specialist. If they claimed to be certified and were not, they would face legal penalties determined by the state. They could, however, legally perform the operation with the patient's consent. Under a regime of certification, the consumer of the service could have the surgery completed by either a certified brain surgeon, pediatrician, or a medical technician who has access to the latest technology on brain surgery. Information on all alternatives would be available to the consumer of the service, but medical insurance companies could put constraints on consumer decisions based on their knowledge of the procedure and legal liability issues. A central policy question for occupational licensing is to what extent the government should protect the consumer against bad decisions.

A further example involves the construction business in Minnesota, where crane operators are licensed. Construction firms that need a crane operator must use a licensed one or none at all. Under certification, only properly credentialed individuals could call themselves certified crane operators, and the state would be responsible for maintaining the list of individuals who have the appropriate skills and current knowledge for the job. However, the construction company would have the ultimate responsibility of assessing the appropriate level of skill required to do the job, and whether to choose a certified operator or someone with lesser skills. This is analogous to construction companies choosing whether or not to hire a union worker on a construction project. The union worker usually has greater skills through the attendance at union-sponsored training programs. Nevertheless, the construction company may choose to go with a nonunion worker, who has lesser skills but may work for substantially less money. The likelihood that a construction company would have the resources to search for the kind of skills required to perform the position is high. Although the question of asymmetric information is important and relevant for individuals who may not have access to the kinds of skills required to do a job, organizations like hospitals, schools, and construction firms are likely to be able to gather the kind of information to make economically rational decisions about the type of labor they require. Finally, under a regime of certification, individuals who misrepresented their education or skills still would be subject to legal penalties under fraud statutes. Yet, the consumer would have greater freedom to choose the appropriate level of skills needed to perform the task. Legal constraints on dental offices, such as mandating that dentists be on site for a dental cleaning or having dental assistants perform different work than hygienists, would not be required by law.

Organizations such as universities can use certification rather than licensing in their hiring decisions, unlike public schools. This gives universities the option of hiring non-PhDs, which is the general educational entry requirement for positions such as faculty or administrators.

Professional schools, such as business schools or schools of public policy, have the ability to hire individuals without the generally accepted qualifications because university professors are not licensed.[2] In contrast, public schools, which require licensing for all teachers and most administrators, do not allow for the flexibility of having unlicensed "professionals."

If certification provides more choices than licensing for consumers, then why not provide just a list of qualified applicants through registration, which is the most lenient form of regulation? Although registration provides the greatest number of choices, it gives only minimal protection for consumers of services where incompetence may lead to major financial or health losses. A list of practitioners similar to those maintained by the Better Business Bureau provides some protection but has little enforcement powers beyond moral suasion. A central monitoring authority like the state, which screens potential applicants, provides greater assurance about the abilities of the individual. Without enforceable costs to violators for "title protection," little quality assurance could be provided to the public on this listing of practitioners. The cost of being removed from the list of registered practitioners without the additional legal penalties for having "inappropriate skills" or for incompetence may lead to insufficient consumer knowledge of the quality of the skill for important services. Without the legal costs inposed by "title infringement," there would be little economic incentives for honesty among service providers. Furthermore, registration may not provide sufficient protection for providers of the occupation to undertake the investments that are required to advance the field. If low-quality practitioners can claim to have the skills and expertise to perform a task, then optimal investments in human capital acquisition may not take place. Unlike registration, certification allows consumers to select only those persons who have met the "certification requirements" established by the profession or any other services, and it allows for the purchase of lower-quality service but without the "brand." The market-based alternative under certification can serve as an incentive for the professions to keep barriers to entry minimal, but meet quality standards. Certification also allows the members of the occupation input into setting entry requirements and continuing education but with the discipline established by the service market.

Recently the solar power industry debated whether to seek licensure or certification for the purveyors of its engineering services for solar powered energy. The report for the industry came to the following conclusion:

> The evidence leads to the conclusion that voluntary national certification for practitioners represents the most beneficial option for the solar industry. Of the various regulatory options, only certification maintains freedom of choice for both consumers and practitioners and has the potential to provide the same quality of installation benefits as state-by-state licensure without imposing the restrictions and higher costs inherent in mandatory licensure (Parker, Bower, and Weissman 2002).

With the recent research on the institution of occupational regulation, policymakers would do well to reconsider the toughest form of regulation that creates monopolies. At the other end of the continuum, just providing a list of potentially qualified individuals with no ratings of their skill level (registration) does not provide enough information to consumers from a perceived impartial monitoring source like the government. The middle-ground of certification gives consumers more information about the training and skill of the practitioner and encourages individuals to seek greater investment in occupation-specific human capital. Moreover, it gives the consumer the ability to choose the appropriate level of expertise they require for the task, and it avoids the issue of finding the proper venue for one occupation over another in performing a task. As in the story of Goldilocks and the Three Bears, where the first one was too hot, the second too cold, and the third one was just right, certification may provide the optimal policy choice of regulation of occupations.

Nevertheless, if occupational licensing is the choice of the public as the optimal way of regulating the workforce, what are the methods to ensure that the occupations are less likely to show the monopoly face of regulation? Shimberg (1982) developed several guides both for the public and for legislators on minimizing the monopoly effects of licensing. He initially proposed many of the questions presented in Appendix A that are now central for any occupation seeking regulation in Minnesota and many other states. However, many of his recommendations on publicizing the complaint rates to licensing boards and the disposition of the complaints to include whether individuals lose their license form a low-cost method of informing the public of the effectiveness of this institution. Moreover, Shimberg's conclusion that licensing has "more bark than bite" is consistent with several of the findings in this book. Just as public universities have only public members on their boards of directors and generally no faculty to oversee the activities of the enterprise, it is important that licensing boards have public members nominated who have been given wide publicity as to their potential appointment so that they are open to "blogger" scrutiny. This would allow interested parties to comment on their suitability for board membership. Members of the profession would then advise the board regarding technical issues within the occupation (Broscheid and Teske 2003). Providing more public involvement, monitoring, and control of licensing may be a second best alternative to certification.

Prospects for Further Research

Although the estimates in this book provide an empirical examination of occupational licensing, there is a greater need to track the growth of regulated and unregulated occupations. Much like the current data effort that is used to track union membership, similar data are needed to follow the growth of occupational licensing. Asking questions in monthly or yearly samples in the CPS and NLSY would enhance analysts' abilities to track the labor market effects of government regulation.

If one of the key issues for the public acceptance of licensing is its ability to avoid "loss aversion," then experiments such as those in the development of prospect theory should be implemented. To what extent are consumers willing to pay for licensing if there is a perception that it reduces downside risks? How many consumers are unwilling to go to an unlicensed practitioner at a discounted price? If certification were a policy option, would there be a regulatory wage or quality premium? Evidence from experimental economics may be helpful in explaining the continuing growth of this labor market institution.

At the international level, even though the data from the United States could use much improvement, the access to EU licensing data would greatly improve the ability of analysts to examine whether labor market regulation matters across international borders. The ability to have international trade in services the way goods are traded may have similar benefits to consumers. Moreover, can occupations move from being regulated to unregulated in the United States similar to what has occurred in Germany (Miller 2004)?

For any of these changes to take place in public policy and data collection and analysis, licensing has to appear on the radar screen of both academics and policymakers. Unlike unions, whose strike or lock-out activity engages local and national attention, policies passed by legislatures on occupational licensing are back-burner issues. Until this form of labor market regulation is shown to have large effects on public expenditures, private sector purchases, or a visible political champion in the policy arena, much of the data that are needed to further gauge and monitor this public policy issue will not be forthcoming, to the detriment of many practitioners, workers, consumers, and the public.

Notes

1. A closed-shop labor agreement means that the employer can only hire employees who are members of the union. These agreements are illegal outside the construction industry under the Taft-Hartley amendments to the National Labor Relations Act, amended (1960).
2. The Public Policy School at the University of Minnesota hired its dean in 2002 without any graduate degrees and granted him full professor status with tenure. In contrast, the Minneapolis Public Schools made its superintendent, who had a PhD in education, take required education classes in Minnesota to become a fully licensed teacher/administrator in the state in order to remain in her position (Brandt 2005).

Appendix A

Criteria for Regulating Occupations for Legislators and a Questionnaire for Occupations Seeking Regulation in Minnesota

Table A.1 A Report to be Completed by Legislators to Comply with Minnesota Statutes on the Criteria for Regulating Occupations

1. What harm will result to the public or could be posed by unregulated practice of the occupation or by continued practice at its current degree of regulation?

2. Is there any reason why existing civil or criminal laws or procedures are inadequate to prevent or remedy any harm to the public?

3. Why is the proposed level of regulation being proposed and why, if there is a lesser degree of regulation, was it not selected?

4. List any associations, organizations, or other groups representing the occupation seeking regulation and the approximate numbers in each in Minnesota.

5. What are the functions typically performed by members of this occupational group, and are they identical or similar to those performed by another occupational group or groups?

6. Is any specialization, training, education, or experience required to engage in the occupation, and if so, how have current practitioners acquired that training, education, and experience?

7. Would the proposed regulation change the way practitioners of the occupation acquire any necessary specialized training, education, or experience, and if so, why?

8. Do any current practitioners of the occupation in Minnesota lack whatever specialized training, education, or experience that might be required to engage in the occupation, and if so, how would the proposed regulation address that lack of training?

9. Would new entrants into the occupation be required to provide evidence of any necessary training, education, or experience, or to pass an examination, or both?

10. Would current practitioners be required to provide evidence of any necessary training, education, or experience, or to pass an examination if the occupation became licensed, and if not, why not?

11. What is the expected impact of the proposed regulation on the supply of practitioners of the occupation and on the cost of services or goods provided by the occupation?

SOURCE: Broat et al. (2004).

**Table A.2 Questionnaire for Proponents of Licensing an Occupation
in Minnesota**

1. Describe the professional or occupational group proposed for regulation
   or expansion of regulation. Include the number of individuals or business
   entities that would be subject to regulation, the names and addresses of
   associations, organizations, and other groups representing practitioners.
   Estimate the number of practitioners in each group.

2. Describe the functions typically performed by members of the occupational group. Indicate the functions performed by this occupational group
   which are similar to those performed by other occupational groups.

3. What functions performed by the occupational group are unsupervised?
   What are typical work settings?

4. Describe any levels of practitioner specialization and qualifications for
   each. Describe the minimum qualifications for entry into the occupation.
   Is there a state or national examination currently used for entry? Is the
   occupation affiliated with an association which enacts and enforces standards? Explain the association's enforcement mechanisms in instances of
   practitioner noncompliance with established standards. State why these efforts are inadequate to protect the public.

5. Is there any state or local business, facility, or industry regulation that can
   protect consumers or clients?

6. Describe and document the physical, emotional, social, or financial consequences to the consumer that result from erroneous or incompetent care/
   practice or omission of appropriate care/practice. Include a description of
   any complaints filed with state law enforcement authorities, courts, de-
   partmental agencies, or other associations that have been lodged against
   practitioners of the profession or occupation in Minnesota within the past
   five years.

7. Describe which existing legal remedies are inadequate to prevent or re-
   dress the kinds of harm that could result from nonregulation. How can
   regulation be provided through an existing state agency or in conjunction
   with presently regulated practitioners?

8. What is the expected impact of the proposed regulation on the existing
   supply of practitioners? What percentage of current practitioners will be
   able to meet the proposed eligibility criteria? If current practitioners will
   be "grandparented," describe how long and under what conditions.

9. Describe the extent to which regulation or expansion of regulation will increase the cost of goods or services provided by practitioners and the overall cost-effectiveness and economic impact of the proposed regulation, including indirect costs to consumers. If applicable, does the profession or occupation plan to apply for mandated benefit coverage?

SOURCE: Broat et al. (2004).

Appendix B

Data Sources

The sources of much of the data used in this book are given along with the years of the surveys and their frequency. In addition, sample sizes for the data are presented along with the sources' unique characteristics that make them useful for analyzing occupational regulation.

Data Used to Analyze Occupational Licensing in the United States

Census of the Population

- Conducted by: U.S. Department of Commerce, U.S. Census Bureau as provided by the Minnesota Population Center (Integrated Public Use Microdata Series), University of Minnesota.
- Survey years: Every 10 years dating to the founding of the United States.
- Unit surveyed: Individuals by household.
- Number of units in survey: Between 5 and 100 percent of the population, depending on the question.
- Unique characteristics: Provides large samples of individuals' labor force status (employed, wages, earnings), demographic characteristics, industry and occupation, national origin, and area of residence.

Current Population Survey (CPS)

- Conducted by: U.S. Department of Commerce, U.S. Census Bureau for the U.S. Department of Labor, Bureau of Labor Statistics.
- Survey years: Monthly since 1943.
- Unit surveyed: Individuals 16 years or older by household.
- Number of units in survey: Approximately 120,000 individuals in 60,000 households.
- Unique characteristics: Each CPS survey includes data on demographic characteristics, labor force status, industry, region, state, and occupation.

U.S. Department of Labor Listing of Licensed Occupations

- Conducted by: U.S. Department of Labor in conjunction with state labor market information agencies.

163

- Survey years: Various years including 2000.
- Units surveyed: State agencies responsible for occupational regulation.
- Unique characteristics: Census of state licensed occupations in the United States as provided to the U.S. Department of Labor in 2000 and updated by state agencies responsible for labor market information and licensing occupations.

Malpractice Insurance Premiums by State for Various Occupations

- Conducted by: Scott Cordes and Yinying Wang for the Center for Labor Policy at the University of Minnesota.
- Survey years: 2004–2005.
- Units surveyed: Insurance companies offering malpractice insurance in all 50 states to pastoral counselors, marriage and family therapists and professional counselors for 2005, and occupational therapists and practical and vocational nurses for 2004.
- Unique characteristics: Rates offered by insurance companies for various levels of coverage and policies by age and experience in regulated and unregulated occupations and states.

National Longitudinal Survey

- Conducted by: The National Longitudinal Survey (NLS) is a survey sponsored by the Bureau of Labor Statistics, U.S. Department of Labor, and conducted by the National Opinion Research Center (NORC) at the University of Chicago with assistance from the Center for Human Resource Research (CHRR) at The Ohio State University. The field work is done by the U.S. Census Bureau.
- Survey years: Occasionally since 1965.
- Units surveyed: The current survey consists of a nationally representative sample of approximately 9,000 individuals and their housholds.
- Unique characteristics: The NLS is a set of surveys designed to gather information at multiple points in time on the labor market activities and other significant life events of several groups of men and women. An extensive two-part questionnaire was administered that listed and gathered demographic information on members of the household and on their immediate family members living elsewhere. Youths are interviewed on an annual or biannual basis. Questions are asked about current and former occupations for the year of the survey.

Survey of Licensing Pass Rates

- Conducted by: The Center for Labor Policy, University of Minnesota, Morris Kleiner with Adrienne Howard and Hwikwon Ham.
- Survey years: Various years between 1980 and 2000.
- Units surveyed: State pass rates for dentists, lawyers, and cosmetologists in the 50 U.S. states.
- Unique characteristics: Various year state pass rates for selected occupations. Generally includes only new entrants and not individuals who are moving from another state.

Survey of Licensing Statutes

- Conducted by: The Center for Labor Policy, University of Minnesota, Morris Kleiner with Adrienne Howard and Hwikwon Ham.
- Survey years: Various years between 1980 and 2000.
- Units surveyed: State statutes for accountants, cosmetologists, dentists, lawyers, and teachers in the 50 U.S. states.
- Unique characteristics: Statutory data and changes in laws on age, citizenship, residency, good moral character, special education, graduate education requirements, experience, exam requirements, bachelor's degree requirements, reciprocity requirements with other states or countries.

Survey of New Air Force Recruits on their Dental Health

- Conducted by: U.S. Air Force personnel at Lowry Air Force Base near Denver, Colorado, for the Center for Labor Policy, University of Minnesota, supervised by Morris Kleiner and Robert Kudrle.
- Survey year: 1992.
- Units surveyed: 464 new Air Force recruits from the 50 U.S. states.
- Unique characteristics: Complete information on Air Force recruits' initial dental exam along with time specific demographic and economic characteristics of the new recruits and their households.

Data Used to Analyze Occupational
Licensing in the European Union

France

Labour Force Surveys ("Enquêtes Emploi")

- Conducted by: The National Institute for Statistics and Economic Studies (INSEE, Paris).
- Survey years: 1990–1997.
- Units surveyed: Household data, approximately 15,600 used for the analysis.
- Unique characteristics: Data on demographic characteristics, labor force status, industry, region, metropolitan area, and occupation.

Germany

Acquisition and Application of Occupational Qualifications 1991/92 ("Qualifikation und Berufsverlauf")

- Conducted by: Bundesinstitut für Berufsbildung (BIBB), Berlin; Institut fuer Arbeitsmarkt- und Berufsforschung der Bundesanstalt für Arbeit, Nuernberg.
- Survey years: 1991–1992.
- Units surveyed: 34,277 individuals.
- Unique characteristics: Detailed occupation characteristics linked to demographic and economic data in Germany.

United Kingdom

Labour Force Survey

- Conducted by: Social and Vital Statistics Division of the Office for National Statistics (ONS) on behalf of the Statistical Outputs Group of the ONS.
- Survey years: Quarterly, annual, or biannual since 1979.
- Units surveyed: Data on 60,000 households.
- Unique characteristics: Data on demographic characteristics, labor force status, industry, region, metropolitan area, and occupation.

Appendix C

Occupations Analyzed in the United States Using Multivariate Techniques

Table C.1 Licensed Occupations and Comparable Unlicensed Occupations, by Census Code and Name, 2000

Census number	Occupation
80	Accountants and auditors
100	Computer systems analysts and scientists
120	Actuaries
28	Purchasing agents and buyers, farm products
29	Buyers, wholesale and retail trade, except farm products
33	Purchasing agents and buyers, n.e.c.
124	Miscellaneous mathematical science occupations
306	Physicians
172	Chemists and material science
161	Biological and life scientists
301	Dentists
331	Dental hygienists
230	Preschool and kindergarten teachers
231	Teachers, elementary school
220	Teachers, secondary school
233	Teachers, special education
282	Public relations specialists
176	Clergy
210	Lawyers
211	Judges
180	Economists
186	Miscellaneous social scientists, including sociologists
201	Social workers
450	Barbers
451	Hairdressers and cosmetologists
404	Bartenders
411	Waiters and waitresses
423	Maids and housemen
62	Human resources, training, and labor relations specialists

Table C.1 (continued)

Census number	Occupation
325	Veterinarians
304	Optometrists
312	Podiatrists
313	Registered nurses
305	Pharmacists
243	Librarians
350	Licensed practical and licensed vocational nurses

References

Akerlof, George. 1970. "The Market for Lemons: Qualitative Uncertainty and the Market Mechanism." *Quarterly Journal of Economics* 84(August): 488–500.

American Association for Marriage and Family Therapy. 2005. "About the American Association for Marriage and Family Therapy." http://www .aamft.org/about /Aboutaamft.asp (accessed May 10, 2005).

American Association of Pastoral Counselors. 2005. "About Pastoral Counseling." http://www.aapc.org/about.htm (accessed May 10, 2005).

American Bar Association. 2003. *State Legislative Reports*. Chicago: American Bar Association. http://www.abanet.org/marketresearch/resource.html (accessed August 25, 2005).

American Counseling Association. 2005. "Inside ACA." http://www.counseling .org/AM/ Template.cfm?Section=INSIDE_ACA (accessed May 10, 2005).

American Dental Education Association. 2004. "Center for Public Policy & Advocacy." http://www.adea.org/CPPA_materials/ (accessed August 16, 2005).

American Institute of Certified Public Accountants. 2004. *American Institute of Certified Public Accountants Membership Statistical Highlights*. http:// www.aicpa.org/members/index.htm (accessed August 22, 2005).

American Professional Agency. 2005. "Our Product Line." http://www .americanprofessional.com/products.htm (accessed March 25, 2005).

American Psychological Association. 1999. *Standards for Psychological Testing*. Washington, DC: American Psychological Association.

America's Career InfoNet. 2005. *Licensed Occupations*. http://www.acinet.org/ acinet/licensedoccupations/lois_state.asp?by=occ&nodeid=16 (accessed August 25, 2005).

Anderson, Gary M., Dennis Halcoussis, Linda Johnston, and Anton D. Lowenberg. 2000. "Regulatory Barriers to Entry in the Healthcare Industry: The Case of Alternative Medicine." *The Quarterly Review of Economics and Finance* 40(4): 485–502.

Andrich, David. 1988. *Rasch Models for Measurement*. Thousand Oaks, CA: Sage Publications.

Angrist, Joshua, and Jonathan Guryan. 2003. "Does Teacher Testing Raise Teacher Quality? Evidence from State Certification Requirements." NBER working paper no. 9545. Cambridge, MA: National Bureau of Economic Research.

Arrow, Kenneth. 1971. *Essays in the Theory of Risk-Bearing*. Chicago: Markham Publishing Co.

Attanasio, Orazio, Gabriella Berloffa, Richard Blundell, and Ian Preston. 2002. "From Earnings Inequality to Consumption Inequality." *Economic Journal* 112(478): C52–C59.

Ballou, Dale, and Michael Podgursky. 1998. "Teacher Recruitment and Retention in Public and Private Schools." *Journal of Policy Analysis and Management* 17(3): 393–417.

———. 2000. "Gaining Control of Professional Licensing and Advancement." In *Conflicting Missions? Teacher Unions and Educational Reform*, Tom Loveless, ed. Washington, DC: Brookings Institution, pp. 69–109.

Bartholomew, David. 1996. *The Statistical Approach to Social Measurement.* London: Academic Press.

Benham, Lee. 1972. "The Effect of Advertising on the Price of Eyeglasses." *Journal of Law and Economics* 15(2): 337–352.

———. 1980. "The Demand for Occupational Licensure." In *Occupational Licensure and Regulation*, Simon Rottenberg, ed. Washington, DC: American Enterprise Institute for Public Policy Research, pp. 13–25.

Berry, Fances, S. 1986. "State Regulation of Occupations and Professions." Lexington, KY: Council of State Governments.

Bertrand, Marianne, and Francis Kramarz. 2001. "Does Entry Restrictions Hinder Job Creation: Evidence from the French Retail Industry." NBER working paper no. 8211. Cambridge, MA: National Bureau of Economic Research.

Biggar, Darryl R., and Michael Owen Wise. 2000. "Competition in Professional Services." OECD, Best Practice Roundtables in Competition Policy No. 27. Paris: Organisation for Economic Co-operation and Development

Blanchflower, David G., and Alex Bryson. 2003. "What Effect Do Unions Have on Wages Now and Would 'What Do Unions Do' be Surprised?" NBER working paper no. 9395. Cambridge, MA: National Bureau of Economic Research.

Blanchflower, David G., and Richard B. Freeman. 1992. "Unionism in the United States and Other Advanced OECD Countries." In *Labor Market Institutions and the Future Role of Unions*, Mario Bognanno and Morris M. Kleiner, eds. Cambridge, MA: Blackwell Press, pp. 56–79.

Bond, Ronald S., John E. Kwoka Jr., John J. Phelan, and Ira Taylor Whitten. 1980. *Effects of Restrictions on Advertising and Commercial Practice in the Professions: The Case of Optometry.* Staff Report, Bureau of Economics, Federal Trade Commission. Washington, DC: U.S. Government Printing Office.

Boulier, Bryan L. 1980. "An Empirical Examination of the Influence of Licensure and Licensure Reform on the Geographical Distribution of Dentists." In *Occupational Licensure and Regulation*, Simon Rottenberg, ed. Washington, DC: American Enterprise Institute for Public Policy Research, pp. 73–97.

Brandt, Steve. 2005. "Peebles Given License Variance." *Star Tribune*, February 3. http://www.parentsunitednetwork.org/4Feb200511.html (accessed August 15, 2005).

Brinegar, Pamela L., and Kara L. Schmitt. 1992. "State Occupational and Professional Licensure." *The Book of the States*, 1992–1993. Lexington, KY: The Council of State Governments, pp. 567–580.

Broat, Alexandra, Neil Chaffee, Devin Grdinic, Leila Kietzman, John Lindner, Clint Pecenka, Matt Schmit, Justin Vander Vegt, and Marie Zimmerman. 2004. *Rethinking Occupational Regulation: A Program Evaluation Report*. A report prepared for the Office of the Legislative Auditor. St. Paul, MN: State of Minnesota.

Broscheid, Andreas, and Paul E. Teske. 2003. "Public Members on Medical Licensing Boards and the Choice of Entry Barriers." *Public Choice* 114(3–4): 445–459.

Budd, John, and Brian P. McCall. 2001. "The Grocery Stores Wage Distribution: A Semi–Parametric Analysis of the Role of Retailing and Labor Market Institutions." *Industrial and Labor Relations Review* 54(2): 484–501.

Bureau of Labor Statistics. 1979. *Handbook of Labor Statistics* 1978. Washington, DC: U.S. Department of Labor.

Busse, Reinhard, and Annette Riesberg. 2004. *Health Care Systems in Transition: Germany*. Copenhagen: WHO Regional Office for Europe on behalf of the European Observatory on Health Systems and Policies.

Cady, John F. 1976. *Restricted Advertising and Competition: The Case of Retail Drugs*. Washington, DC: American Enterprise Institute.

Camerer, Colin, Samuel Issacharoff, George Loewenstein, Ted O'Donoghue, and Matthew Rabin. 2003. "Regulation for Conservatives: Behavioral Economics and the Case for 'Asymmetric Paternalism.'" *University of Pennsylvania Law Review* 151(3): 1211–1254.

Carman, H.G. 1958. "The Historical Development of Licensing for the Professions." *The Educational Record* 39: 268–278.

Carroll, Sidney L., and Robert J. Gaston. 1981. "Occupational Restrictions and the Quality of Service Received: Some Evidence." *Southern Economic Journal* 47(4): 959–976.

Clarkson, Kenneth, and Timothy J. Muris. 1980. "The Federal Trade Commission and Occupational Regulation." In *Occupational Licensing and Regulation*, Simon Rottenberg, ed. Washington, DC: American Enterprise Institute for Public Policy Research, pp. 107–141.

Commission of the European Communities. 2004. *Report on Competition in Professional Services*. Brussels: Commission of the European Communities.

Committee on Competition Law and Policy. 2000. *Competition in Professional Services*. Paris: Organisation for Economic Co-operation and Development.

Commonwealth Fund. 2002. *2002 International Health Policy Survey of Adults with Health Problems*. New York: Commonwealth Fund. http://www.cmwf.org/surveys/surveys_show.htm?doc_id=228168 (accessed August 12, 2005).

Conrad, Douglas A., and George G. Sheldon. 1982. "The Effects of Legal Constraints on Dental Care Prices." *Inquiry* 19(1): 51–67.

Cordes, Scott. 2005. "The Impact of Occupational Licensure on Malpractice Premiums in Selected Mental Health Professions." Unpublished M.A. thesis, Humphrey Institute of Public Affairs, University of Minnesota.

Council on Licensure, Enforcement, and Regulation (CLEAR). 2004. "CLEAR's Mission and Purpose." http://www.clearhq.org/mission_and_vision.htm (accessed July 22, 2005).

Council of State Governments. 1952. *Occupational Licensing Legislation in the States*. Chicago, IL: Council of State Governments.

Cox, Carolyn, and Susan Foster. 1990. *The Costs and Benefits of Occupational Regulation*. Washington, DC: Bureau of Economics, Federal Trade Commission. Washington, DC: U.S. Government Printing Office.

Cutler David M., and Ernst R. Berndt. 2001. "Introduction." In *Medical Care Output and Productivity*, David M. Cutler and Ernst R. Berndt, eds. Chicago: University of Chicago Press, pp. 1–11.

Dent v. West Virginia, 129 U.S. 114 (1888).

DiNardo, John, Nicole Fortin, and Thomas Lemieux. 1996. "Labor Market Institutions and the Distribution of Wages, 1973–1992: A Semi–Parametric Approach." *Econometrica* 64(5): 1001–1044.

Dunlop, John T. 1993. *Industrial Relations Systems*. Boston: Harvard Business School Press.

Eckstein, Zvi, and Eva Nagypal. 2004. "The Evolution of U.S. Earnings Inequality: 1961–2002." *Federal Reserve Bank of Minneapolis Quarterly Review* 28(2): 10–29.

Ehrenreich, Barbara, and Deirdre English. 1973. *Witches, Midwives, and Nurses: A History of Women Healers*. Old Westbury, NY: Feminist Press.

Federal Trade Commission. 2002. "Declaratory Ruling Proceeding on the Interpretation and Applicability of Various Statutes and Regulations Concerning the Sale of Contact Lenses." Office of Policy Planning and the Bureau of Consumer Protection. Washington, DC: Federal Trade Commission.

Feldman, Roger, and James W. Begun. 1978. "The Effects of Advertising: Lessons from Optometry." *Journal of Human Resources* 13(Supplement): 247–262.

————. 1980. "Does Advertising of Prices Reduce the Mean and Variance of Prices?" *Economic Inquiry* 18(3): 487–492.

Field, Marilyn, ed. 1995. *Dental Education at the Crossroads: Challenges and Change.* Washington, DC: National Academy of Sciences.

Filer, Randal, Daniel Hammermesh, and Albert Rees. 1994. *The Economics of Work and Pay.* New York: Harper and Row.

Fixler, Dennis, and Mitchell Ginsburg. 2001. "Health Care Output and Prices in the Producer Price Index." In *Medical Care Output and Productivity,* David M. Cutler and Ernst R. Berndt, eds. Chicago, IL: University of Chicago Press.

Ford, Ina Kay, and Daniel H. Ginsburg. 2001. "Medical Care in the Consumer Price Index." In *Medical Care Output and Productivity,* David M. Cutler and Ernst R. Berndt, eds. Chicago, IL: University of Chicago Press, pp. 203–219.

Fossum, John A. 2002. *Labor Relations: Development, Structure, Process.* Boston: McGraw-Hill.

Frank, Robert. 1988, "Bureaucratic Turfbuilding in a Rational World." *European Journal of Political Economy* 4(Supplementary Issue): 65–75.

Freeman, Richard, and Morris M. Kleiner. 1990. "The Impact of New Unionization on Wages and Working Conditions." *Journal of Labor Economics* 8(1, pt 2): S8–S25.

Freeman, Richard B., and Edward P. Lazear. 1995. "An Economic Analysis of Works Councils." In *Works Councils: Consultation, Representation, and Cooperation in Industrial Relations,* Joel Rogers and Wolfgang Streek, eds. Chicago: University of Chicago Press, pp. 27–50.

Freeman, Richard B., and James Medoff. 1984. *What Do Unions Do?* New York: Basic Books.

Friedman, Lawrence. 1965. "Freedom of Contract and Occupational Licensing, 1890–1910: A Legal and Social Study." *California Law Review* 53: 487–534.

Friedman, Milton. 1962a. *Capitalism and Freedom.* Chicago: University of Chicago Press.

————. 1962b. *Price Theory: A Provisional Text.* Chicago: Aldine.

Friedman, Milton, and Simon Kuznets. 1945. *Income from Independent Professional Practice.* New York: National Bureau of Economic Research.

Garoupa, Nuno. 2004. "Regulation of Professions in the U.S. and Europe: A Comparative Analysis." Paper presented at the American Law and Economics Association Fourteenth Annual Meeting held in Chicago, May 7–8.

Gellhorn, Walter. 1976. "The Abuse of Occupational Licensing." *University of Chicago Law Review* 44(Fall): 6–27.

Goldfarb v. Virginia 421 U.S. 773 (1975).

Graddy, Elizabeth. 1991. "Interest Groups or the Public Interest—Why Do We Regulate Health Occupations?" *Journal of Health, Politics, Policy and Law* 16(1): 25–49.

Greene, Karen. 1969. *Occupational Licensing and the Supply of Nonprofessional Manpower*. Washington, DC: Manpower Administration, U.S. Department of Labor.

Gross, Stanley. 1984. *Of Foxes and Hen Houses: Licensing and the Health Professions*. Westport, CT: Quorum Books.

Haas-Wilson, Deborah. 1986. "The Effect of Commercial Practice Restrictions: The Case of Optometry." *Journal of Law and Economics* 29(1): 165–186.

Hagen, Mindy. 2001. "Bracing for the Future." *Northwestern Daily*, May 14. http://flouoride.oralhealth.org/papers/2001/northwesternclose.htm (accessed August 12, 2005).

Hallman, Ben. 2004. "Dental Workers Oppose Change in Rules: Hygienists Say Allowing Assistants to Clean Teeth Is Bad for Patients." *St. Louis Post–Dispatch*, February 11, C:1.

Hammermesh, Daniel. 1993. *Labor Demand*. Princeton, NJ: Princeton University Press.

Heckman, James. 1979. "Sample Selection Bias as a Specification Error." *Econometrica* 47(1): 153–162.

Hirsch, Barry, and David Macpherson. 2005. Unionstats.com: Union Membership and Coverage Database from the CPS (Documentation). http://www.unionstats.com (accessed October 5, 2005).

Hirschman, Albert. 1970. *Exit, Voice and Loyalty*. Cambridge, MA: Harvard University Press.

Holen, Arlene S. 1978. *The Economics of Dental Licensing*. Arlington, VA: Public Research Institute of the Center for Naval Analysis.

Hollings, Robert L., and Christal Pike-Nase. 1997. *Professional and Occupational Licensure in the United States: An Annotated Bibliography and Professional Resource*. Westport, CT: Greenwood Press.

Iannaccone, Laurence R. 1992. "Sacrifice and Stigma: Reducing Free–riding in Cults, Communes, and Other Collectives." *Journal of Political Economy* 100(2): 271–291.

International Federation of Social Workers. 2004. "Registration of Social Work: Review of Status across Member Organisations." http://www.ifsw.org/GM-2004 /RegistrationSurvey.pdf (accessed August 25, 2005).

Jeffery, Mark. 2001. "The Free Movement of Persons within the European Union: Moving from Employment Rights to Fundamental Rights?" *Comparative Labor Law & Policy Journal* 23(1): 211–232.

Jetha, Sajaad A. 2002. "The Economics of Occupational Licensing and Dental Practitioners." M.A. Thesis. London School of Economics.

Kahneman, Daniel, J. Knetsch, and R. Thaler. 1991. "The Endowment Effect, Loss Aversion, and Status Quo Bias." *Journal of Economic Perspectives* 5(1): 193–206.

Kahneman, Daniel, and Richard Thaler. 1991. "Economic Analysis and the Psychology of Utility: Applications to Compensation Policy." *American Economic Review* 81(2): 341–352.

Kahneman, Daniel, and Amos Tversky. 1979. "Prospect Theory: An Analysis of Decisions under Risk." *Econometrica* 47(2): 263–291.

Kandel, Eugene, and Edward Lazear. 1992. "Peer Pressure and Partnerships." *Journal of Political Economy* 100(4): 801–817.

Kane, Thomas J., Jonah E. Rockoff, and Douglas O. Staiger. 2005. "Identifying Effective Teachers in New York City." An unpublished paper presented at the NBER Summer Institute, Cambridge, MA, July 28.

Kane, Thomas J., and Douglas O. Staiger. 2005. "Using Imperfect Information to Identify Effective Teachers." Unpublished manuscript.

Kleiner, Morris, M. 1990. "Are There Economic Rents for More Restrictive Occupational Licensing Practices?" In *Industrial Relations Research Association Proceedings*, Madison, WI: Industrial Relations Research Association, pp. 177–185.

———. 2000. "Occupational Licensing." *Journal of Economic Perspectives* 14(4): 189–202.

———. 2002. *Occupational Licensing and the Internet: Issues for Policy Makers.* A report prepared for the Federal Trade Commission, Washington, DC, October 1. www.ftc.gov/opp/ecommerce/anticompetitive/panel/kleiner.pdf (accessed August 8, 2005).

———. 2003. *Occupational Licensing and Health Services: Who Gains and Who Loses?* A report prepared for the Federal Trade Commission, Washington, DC, June 10. www.ftc.gov/ogc/healthcarehearings/docs/030610kleiner.pdf (accessed August 8, 2005).

Kleiner, Morris M., Robert S. Gay, and Karen Greene. 1982. "Barriers to Labor Migration: The Case of Occupational Licensing." *Industrial Relations* 21(3): 383–391.

Kleiner, Morris M., and Mitchell Gordon. 1996. "The Growth of Occupational Licensing: Are We Protecting Consumers?" *Center for Urban and Regional Affairs Reporter* 26(4): 8–12.

Kleiner, Morris M., and Robert T. Kudrle. 2000. "Does Regulation Affect Economic Outcomes? The Case of Dentistry." *The Journal of Law and Economics* 43(2): 547–582.

Kleiner, Morris M., and Daniel L. Petree. 1988. "Unionism and Licensing of Public School Teachers: Impact on Wages and Educational Output." In

When Public Sector Workers Unionize, Richard B. Freeman and Casey Ich-niowski, eds. Chicago: University of Chicago Press, pp. 305–319.

Krueger, Alan. 2000. "From Bismarck to Maastricht: The March to European Union and the Labor Compact." NBER working paper no. 7456. Cam-bridge, MA: National Bureau of Economic Research.

Kugler, Adrianna D., and Robert M. Sauer. 2005. "Doctors Without Borders? Relicensing Requirements and Negative Selection in the Market for Physi-cians." *Journal of Labor Economics* 23(3): 437–465.

Kwoka, John E., Jr. 1984. "Advertising and the Price and Quality of Optomet-ric Services." *American Economic Review* 74(1): 211–216.

Law, Marc, and Sukko Kim. 2004. "Specialization and Regulation: The Rise of Professionals and the Emergence of Occupational Licensing Regulation," NBER working paper no. 10467. Cambridge, MA: National Bureau of Eco-nomic Research.

Leland, Hayne. 1979. "Quacks, Lemons, and Licensing: A Theory of Mini-mum Quality Standards." *Journal of Political Economy* 87(6): 1328–1346.

Lewis, H. Gregg, ed. 1962. *Aspects of Labor Economics*. Princeton, NJ: Prince-ton University Press.

———. 1986. *Union Relative Wage Effects: A Survey*. Chicago: University of Chicago Press.

Liang, J. Nellie, and Jonathan D. Ogur. 1987. *Restrictions on Dental Auxilia-ries*. Washington, DC: Federal Trade Commission.

Lonbay, Julian. 2004. "The Free Movement of Persons." *International and Comparative Law Quarterly* 53(2): 479–487.

Maurizi, Alex R. 1974. "Occupational Licensing and the Public Interest." *Journal of Political Economy* 82(2): 399–413.

———. 1980. "The Impact of Regulation of Quality: the Case of California Contractors." In *Occupational Licensure and Regulation*, Simon Rotten-berg, ed. Washington, DC: American Enterprise Institute for Public Policy Research, pp. 399–413.

Miller, John. 2004. "Europe's 'Outdated' Job Rules: Some Say Certification Requirements Hinder EU Productivity." *Wall Street Journal*, August 16, A:11.

Mincer, Jacob. 1986. "Wage Changes in Job Changes." *Research in Labor Economics* 8(Part A): 171–197.

Minnesota Board of Medical Practice. 1993–2002. *Biennial Reports*. Minne-apolis, MN: Minnesota Board of Medical Practice.

Minnesota House of Representatives. 2004. *Welcome to the Minnesota House of Representatives*. http://www.house.leg.state.mn.us.

Minnesota Legislature, Senate. 2000, 2002. *Journals of the Senate of the Leg-islature of the State of Minnesota*. St. Paul, MN: State of Minnesota.

Minnesota Secretary of State. 1997, 1999, 2001. *Minnesota Legislative Manual.* St. Paul, MN: State of Minnesota.

———. 2004. Minnesota Senate. http://www.senate.leg.state.mn.us.

Nash, Betty Joyce. 2003. "May I See Your License, Please? Excessive Occupational Licensing Can Cost Consumers Money Without Necessarily Increasing Quality or Protection." *Region Focus* (Summer): 25–27. http://www.richmondfed.org/publications/economic_research/region_focus/summer_2003/feature2.cfm (accessed October 10, 2005).

National Institute for Statistics and Economic Studies (INSEE). 1998. *Enquête Emploi.* Paris: French Ministry of the Economy, Finance, and Industry.

Neuman, Shoshana, and Ronald Oaxaca. 2003. "Estimating Labor Market Discrimination with Selection Corrected Wage Equations." Department of Economics working paper. Tel Aviv, Israel: Tel Aviv University.

Office of the Legislative Auditor, State of Minnesota. 1999. *Occupational Regulation: A Program Evaluation Report.* St. Paul, MN: State of Minnesota.

Pagliero, Mario. 2004. "What Is the Objective of Professional Licensing? Evidence from the U.S. Market for Lawyers." PhD Thesis, Department of Economics, London Business School.

Parker v. Brown 317 U.S. 341 (1943).

Parker, Wendy L., Ward Bower, and Jane Weissman. 2002. "Costs and Benefits of Practitioner Certification or Licensure for the Solar Industry." A paper presented at the IEEE PV Specialist Conference held in New Orleans, LA, May 20–24.

Pashigian, B. Peter. 1979. "Occupational Licensing and the Interstate Mobility of Professionals," *Journal of Law and Economics* 22(1): 1–25.

———. 1980. "Has Occupational Licensing Reduced Geographic Mobility and Raised Earnings?" In *Occupational Licensure and Regulation,* Simon Rottenberg, ed. Washington, DC: American Enterprise Institute, pp. 299–333.

Paterson, Iain, Marcel Fink, and Anthony Ogus. 2003. *Economic Impact of Regulation in the Field of Liberal Professions in Different Member States: Regulation of Professional Services.* Vienna, Austria: Institute for Advanced Studies.

Paul, Chris. 1984. "Physician Licensure Legislation and the Quality of Medical Care." *Atlantic Economic Journal* 12(4): 18–30.

Perloff, Jeffrey M. 1980. "The Impact of Licensing Laws on Wage Changes in the Construction Industry." *Journal of Law and Economics* 23(2): 409–428.

Phelan, J. 1974. *Regulation of the Television Repair Industry in Louisiana and California: A Case Study.* Washington, DC: Federal Trade Commission.

Pischke, Jorn-Steffen, and Till von Wachter. 2005. "Zero Returns to Compulsory Schooling in Germany: Evidence and Interpretation." NBER working paper no. 11414. Cambridge, MA: National Bureau of Economic Research.

Rademacher, Tom. 1997. "Don't Try This at Home: Man Does Own Root Canals." *Ann Arbor News*, February 9: A:11.

Reed, Danielle. 2005. "States Push Licensing of Mortgage Loan Officers." *Wall Street Journal*, August 16, D:2.

Robinson, Ray, and Anna Dixon. 1999. *Health Care in Transition: United Kingdom.* Copenhagen: WHO Regional Office for Europe on behalf of the European Observatory on Health Systems and Policies.

Rottenberg, Simon. 1980. "Introduction." In *Occupational Licensure and Regulation*, Simon Rottenberg, ed. Washington, DC: American Enterprise Institute for Public Policy Research, pp. 1–10.

Sackett, Paul. 2004. *Conversations with Professor Paul Sackett.* Department of Psychology, University of Minnesota, March 20.

Sandier, Simone, Valerie Paris, and Dominique Polton. 2004. *Health Care Systems in Transition: France.* Copenhagen: WHO Regional Office for Europe on behalf of the European Observatory on Health Systems and Policies.

Scopp, Thomas S. 2003. "The Relationship Between the 1990 Census and Census 2000 Industry and Occupation Systems." Technical paper no. 65. Washington, DC: U.S. Census Bureau.

Scoville, James. 1969. *The Job Content of the US Economy: 1940–1970.* New York: McGraw–Hill.

Shapiro, Carl. 1986. "Investment, Moral Hazard and Occupational Licensing." *Review of Economic Studies* 53(5): 843–862.

Shepard, Lawrence. 1978. "Licensing Restrictions and the Cost of Dental Care." *Journal of Law and Economics* 21(1): 187–201.

Shimberg, Benjamin. 1982. *Occupational Licensing: A Public Perspective.* Princeton, NJ: Educational Testing Service.

Shimberg, Benjamiin, Barbara Esser, and Daniel Kruger. 1973. *Occupational Licensing: Practices and Policies.* Washington, DC: Public Affairs Press.

Siebert, W.S. 1977. "Occupational Licensing: The Merison Report on the Regulation of the Medical Profession." *British Journal of Industrial Relations* 15(1): 29–38.

Simms, Patricia. 2004. "Dental Hygienists Fight State over Cut-Rate Teeth-Whitening Service." *Wisconsin State Journal*, March 17, B:1.

Smith, Adam. 1937. *The Wealth of Nations.* New York: The Modern Library. (Orig. pub. 1776.)

Smith-Peters, Lise, and Bruce Smith-Peters. 1994. *The Directory of Professional and Occupational Regulation in the United States and Canada.* Lexington, KY: Council on Licensure, Enforcement and Regulation.

Spence, Michael. 1973. "Job Market Signaling." *Quarterly Journal of Economics* 87(3): 355–374.

Statistical Office of the European Communities. 2004. "Eurostat." http://europa .eu.int/comm/eurostat/ (accessed August 16, 2005).

Stigler, George. 1971. "The Theory of Economic Regulation." *Bell Journal of Economics and Management Science* 2(1): 3–21.

Studenmund, A.H. 1997. *Using Econometrics: A Practical Guide*. Reading MA: Addison–Wesley.

Sunday Patriot News. 1995. Harrisburg, PA, August 13, B:1.

Tabachnik, L. 1976. "Licensing in the Legal and Medical Professions, 1820–1860: A Historical Case Study." In *Professions for the People: The Politics of Skill*, Joel E. Gerstl and Glenn Jacobs, eds. Cambridge, MA: Schenkman, pp. 25–42.

Tenn, Steven. 2001. "Three Essays on the Relationship between Migration and Occupational Licensing." Unpublished dissertation, Department of Economics, University of Chicago.

Thomas v. Collins 323 U.S. 516, 545 (1945).

Thornton, Robert J., and Andrew Weintraub. 1979. "Licensing in the Barbering Profession." *Industrial and Labor Relations Review* 32(2): 242–249.

Triplett, Jack E. 2001. "What's Different about Health? Human Repair and Car Repair in National Accounts and in National Health Accounts." In *Medical Care Output and Productivity*, David M. Cutler and Ernst R. Berndt, eds. Chicago: University of Chicago Press, pp. 15–94.

U.S. Census Bureau. 2000. *Five-Percent Public Use Microdata Sample*. Washington, DC: U.S. Census Bureau.

———. 2003. *Population of the States*. Washington, DC: U.S. Census Bureau.

Wang, Andrew. 1997. "Economic Reform and State Enterprise Productivity in China: An Application of Robust Estimation and Latent Variable Measurement Methods." PhD Thesis. Harvard University.

Wheelan, Charles J. 1999. "Politics or Public Interest? An Empirical Examination of Occupational Licensure." Unpublished manuscript, Chicago: University of Chicago.

———. 2005. Politics or Public Interest? Licensing and the Case of Respiratory Therapists." *Perspectives on Work* 8(2): 42–43.

White, Lawrence J. 1999. "Reducing the Barriers to International Trade in Accounting Services: Why It Matters, and the Road Ahead." A paper presented at the American Enterprise Institute conference "Services 2000: New Directions in Services Trade Liberalization," held in Washington, DC, June 1–2.

White, William D. 1980. "Mandatory Licensure of Registered Nurses: Introduction and Impact." In *Occupational Licensure and Regulation*, Simon

Rottenberg, ed. Washington, DC: American Enterprise Institute for Public Policy Research, pp. 47–72.

Wholesale Access Mortgage Research and Consulting, Inc. 2005. A presentation to the National Association of Mortgage Brokers annual convention held in Minneapolis, MN, on June 11–14.

Wisconsin Act 67. 1997. http://www.legis.state.wi.us/1997/data/acts/97Act67.pdf (accessed August 12, 2005).

Wisconsin Act 107. 1993. http://www.legis.state.wi.us/acts89-93/93Act107.pdf (accessed August 12, 2005).

Wisconsin Court System. 2005. *Diploma Privilege.* http://www.wicourts.gov/services/attorney/bardiploma.htm (Accessed August 12, 2005).

Wisconsin Department of Regulation and Licensing. 2004, 2005. *Health Professions.* http://drl.wi.gov/prof/burhealth.htm (accessed August 12, 2005).

The Author

Morris M. Kleiner is a professor at the Humphrey Institute of Public Affairs and the Industrial Relations Center at the University of Minnesota–Twin Cities. He is a research associate in Labor Studies at the National Bureau of Economic Research and a visiting scholar in the economic research department at the Federal Reserve Bank of Minneapolis. He has served as an associate in employment policy with the Brookings Institution, a visiting scholar in the Harvard University economics department, and a research fellow at the London School of Economics. He received a PhD in economics from the University of Illinois. He began his research on occupational licensing while at the U.S. Department of Labor in 1976. His analysis of occupational licensing has been supported by the National Science Foundation, the U.S. Department of Labor, and the W.E. Upjohn Institute for Employment Research. He has published extensively on issues of occupational regulation, and has presented his work on this topic at several universities in Europe, Australia, and the United States. In addition, Professor Kleiner has provided advice on occupation regulation policy to the Federal Trade Commission, the Department of Justice, state legislatures, and occupation associations.

Index

The italic letters *f, n,* and *t* following a page number indicate that the subject information of the heading is within a figure, note, or table, respectively, on that page.

About the Institute

The W.E. Upjohn Institute for Employment Research is a nonprofit research organization devoted to finding and promoting solutions to employment-related problems at the national, state, and local levels. It is an activity of the W.E. Upjohn Unemployment Trustee Corporation, which was established in 1932 to administer a fund set aside by Dr. W.E. Upjohn, founder of The Upjohn Company, to seek ways to counteract the loss of employment income during economic downturns.

The Institute is funded largely by income from the W.E. Upjohn Unemployment Trust, supplemented by outside grants, contracts, and sales of publications. Activities of the Institute comprise the following elements: 1) a research program conducted by a resident staff of professional social scientists; 2) a competitive grant program, which expands and complements the internal research program by providing financial support to researchers outside the Institute; 3) a publications program, which provides the major vehicle for disseminating the research of staff and grantees, as well as other selected works in the field; and 4) an Employment Management Services division, which manages most of the publicly funded employment and training programs in the local area.

The broad objectives of the Institute's research, grant, and publication programs are to 1) promote scholarship and experimentation on issues of public and private employment and unemployment policy, and 2) make knowledge and scholarship relevant and useful to policymakers in their pursuit of solutions to employment and unemployment problems.

Current areas of concentration for these programs include causes, consequences, and measures to alleviate unemployment; social insurance and income maintenance programs; compensation; workforce quality; work arrangements; family labor issues; labor-management relations; and regional economic development and local labor markets.